Oh Susannah

Bananas play a key role in this delightful story!

"Susannah looked at her mom and then at the banana. Her backpack was propped against her chair. Holding the banana between her thumb and forefinger, she dropped it into her schoolbag behind her folders that hid her unfinished homework."

From *Oh Susannah*

It all begins with homework trouble and an invitation to a sleepover that she doesn't want to go to in a creepy house. Rather than dealing with her problems, Susannah stuffs them into her backpack. But how much can a backpack take? Will she be able to confront her worries before the backpack bursts? Or will she just continue to hide them away? Join Susannah and her friends in this story sure to charm busy young readers everywhere.

www.caroleproman.com

Banana Bread

Yield 1 loaf

INGREDIENTS

2 cups all-purpose flour
1 tsp baking powder
1 tsp baking soda
½ tsp kosher salt
½ cup unsalted butter, melted
1 cup granulated sugar
1 large egg plus 1 egg yolk
¼ cup sour cream
1 tsp vanilla extract
4 ripe bananas, mashed with a fork
½ cup semi-sweet chocolate chips
½ cup chopped toasted walnuts

Tip: You can freeze the bananas! If you can't use the ripe banana immediately, remove banana from peel and freeze in a freezer bag until ready to use. Defrost before using in recipe.

DIRECTIONS

1. Preheat oven to 350F. Line a loaf pan with parchment paper.
2. In a bowl, whisk together flour, baking soda, baking powder and salt.
3. In a large bowl, mix melted butter, sugar, egg and egg yolk, sour cream, and vanilla. Add mashed bananas and stir until combined. Gradually add dry ingredients to wet ingredients until just combined.
4. Fold in chocolate chips and walnuts and transfer to prepared loaf pan.
5. Bake until a toothpick comes out clean, about 1 hour. Remove from oven and let cool 10 minutes in pan, then turn out onto a cooling rack to cool completely.

Egg free: Use ⅓ cup applesauce in place of eggs.

Piccadilly and the Jolly Raindrops

There is a presence of fairies and yummy cupcakes with rainbow sprinkles throughout the Piccadilly series!

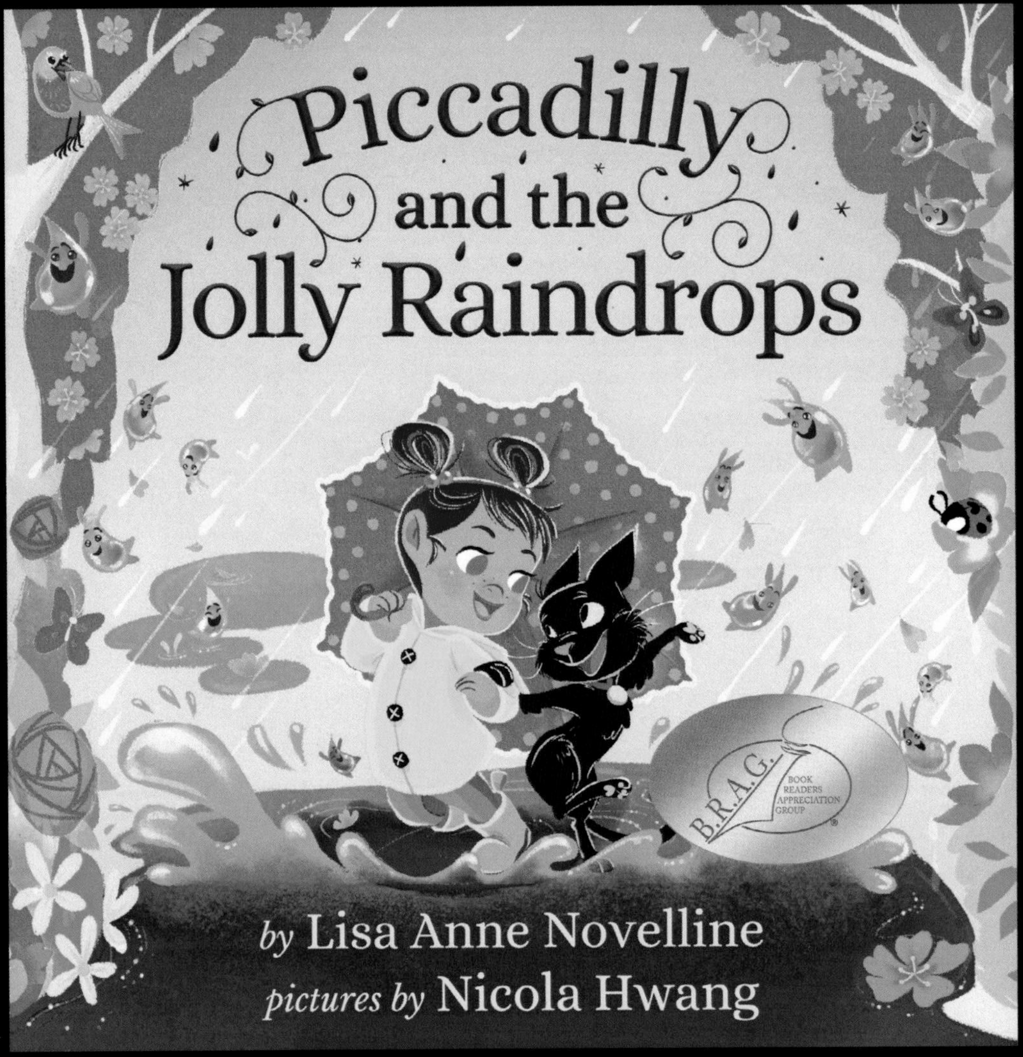

Delight with Piccadilly as she learns to reframe her gloomy afternoon into one of the most fantastic days of her life! Piccadilly and the Jolly Raindrops is a tale of joy and wonder wrapped around one of the mightiest messages of all: children possess the power to choose a positive view of challenges. And when they exercise that power, the most magical of possibilities await!

www.lisaannenovelline.com

Vanilla-Fairy Muffins

Yield 2 dozen

INGREDIENTS

1½ cups unbleached white flour
2 cups whole wheat flour
1 cup sugar
1 tsp baking powder
½ tsp baking soda
¾ tsp salt
2 beaten eggs
1½ cup milk
⅔ cup vegetable oil
1½ tsp vanilla extract
Icing
½ cup butter
2 ½ cups confectioner's sugar
1 tsp vanilla
¼ cup milk
1 tbsp sprinkles of choice

DIRECTIONS

1. Stir together flour, sugar, baking powder, baking soda and salt. Make a well in the center.
2. Combine eggs, milk and oil. Add all at once to dry ingredients, stirring until just moistened.
3. Fill greased muffin pan or paper cup liners. Fill two thirds full and bake at 375F for 15-18 minutes.
4. Cook muffins. Cool. Soften butter. Add confectioner's sugar and cream until light and fluffy. Stir in vanilla. Add milk, a little at a time until the correct consistency is achieved.
5. Ice cupcakes and then scatter with sprinkles of choice.

Sugar Free: Substitute ½ cup sugar substitute in base recipe. Omit icing, dip muffins in melted butter and a brown sugar substitute.

Sofie at Bat

Nothing says "Baseball" better than Hot Dogs!

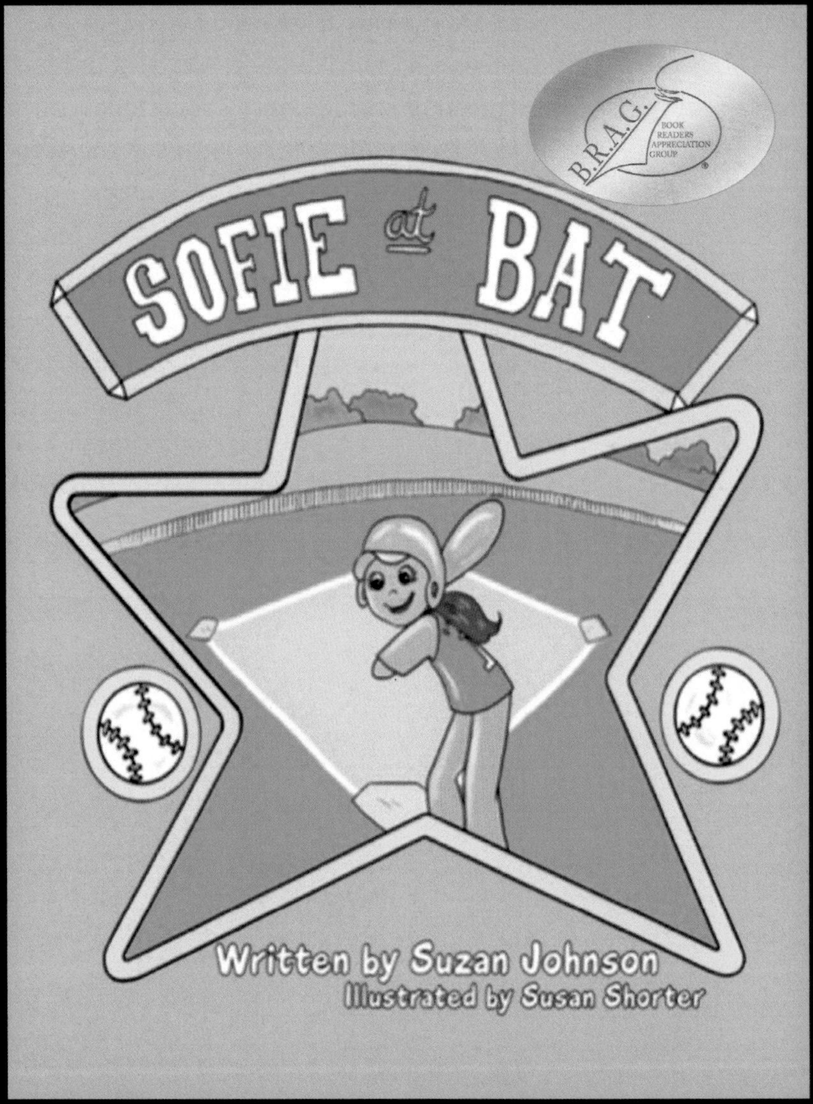

Learn how an eight-year-old girl finds her inner strength. Sofie at Bat will capture the attention of young readers. Prepare to be motivated to try hard, no matter what the outcome may be. Sofie is not able to hit the softball without a tee. With the love and encouragement of her friends and family will Sofie make a hit?

www.shjstories.com

Hot dogs With Toppings

INGREDIENTS

Hot dogs and buns
Classic mustard
Minced onions
Lettuce
Hot peppers
Red bell pepper
Salsa
Jalapeño peppers
Guacamole
Relish
Sauerkraut
Ketchup
Chili
Cheese
Mayonnaise (sriracha infused for heat!)
Avocado

There are so many ways to cook hot dogs – grill them, fry them or broil them. However, most chefs agree, the best way to get the perfect hot dog is to steam them! Steaming brings out that ballpark flavor without drying them out.

DIRECTIONS

Here's how a leading restaurant chain recommends cooking their Hot Dogs-

1. Add water to a skillet or frying pan. Cover the surface with half an inch of water.
2. Turn the heat on medium-high. Heat the pan until the water starts to boil off.
3. Gently add the hot dogs. You'll only want to cook a few at a time with this method.
4. Steam them.

Be creative – set out bowls filled with all the toppings, add some chips, fries or cut veggies and you are all set for a great ball game!

The first book in the Smartee Plate series teaches the importance of eating a variety of fruits AND vegetables, while introducing vocabulary such as vitamins, minerals, antioxidants, and fiber. Meet Theodora (Teddy) Rose, an "almost-six-years-old" girl who loves to garden but hates eating the vegetables she grows. Broccoli? Yuck. Asparagus? Double yuck! Brussels sprouts? No way! Teddy absolutely, no two ways about it, dislikes eating vegetables! But when she stumbles upon a band of fruits and veggies rocking out in her garden, she's in for a delicious adventure.

www.smarteeplate.com

Teddy Tries a Veggie

"Can a singing band of vegetables get Teddy to appreciate all the good food in her garden?"

From *Teddy Tries a Veggie*

Veggie and Fruit Kabobs

INGREDIENTS

Wooden skewers
Cucumber chunks
Cherry tomatoes
Bell pepper chunks
Mushrooms
Zucchini slices
Carrots
Pineapple
Apples
Watermelon
Grapes
Cantaloupe

DIRECTIONS

1. Cut veggies and fruit into 1 to 1½" pieces.
2. Put each piece on a wooden skewer. Refrigerate until serving.
3. Add a dip if desired: try salsa, hummus, guacamole, plain or flavored yoghurt and prepared dressings such as ranch or sweet and sour.

Optional: Add chunks of your favorite cheese to the veggie kabobs.

Tilly and Torg Out To Eat

Tilly and Torg dine out on one of their favorites -Spaghetti & Meatballs! This is a great meal to fix with your kids – just a little supervision and aprons required!

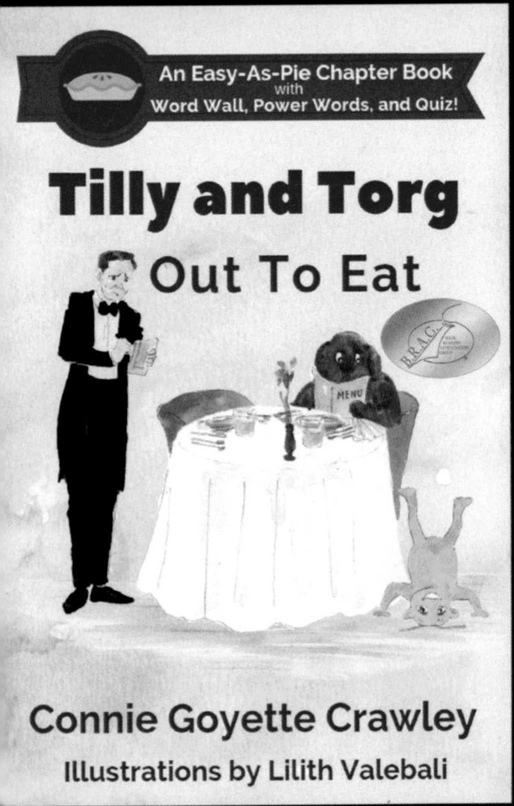

Here come Tilly and Torg! These two hilarious monsters have a lot to learn about living with humans! When there's no food in the house, Tilly and Torg head out to a restaurant – and one thing is for sure! With these two, trouble is always on the menu!

www.conniecrawley.com

Spaghetti and Meatballs

Serves 6

MARINARA SAUCE INGREDIENTS

2 tbsp olive oil
1 medium onion, chopped
3 large cloves garlic, minced
1 green bell pepper, chopped
2 lbs fresh Roma tomatoes, chopped or 1 28 oz can San Marzano whole tomatoes
½ cup dry red wine
1 tsp kosher salt
½ tsp pepper
1 tsp brown sugar
4 sprigs fresh oregano, leaves removed or 1 tsp dried oregano
5-6 fresh basil leaves, chopped or 1 tsp dried basil
2 sprigs fresh parsley, chopped or 1 tsp dried

DIRECTIONS

1. Add onion and olive oil to a saucepan over medium heat and cook until onion is translucent. Add garlic and simmer for 2-3 minutes.
2. Add rest of ingredients. Before putting tomatoes in pot, place in a bowl and break up tomatoes with a wooden spoon or with your hands (Children will love to help break up the tomatoes. Aprons are suggested!) Add tomatoes to pot and stir.
3. Lower heat and simmer for about 45 minutes, stirring occasionally, until sauce has thickened.
4. Taste and adjust seasoning.
5. If you like chunky sauce, leave as is. If you like it smoother, purée with an immerser blender until desired smoothness.

Expandthetable Suggestions:

Make it cheesy: Add Parmesan cheese on top of pasta if desired.

Add some spice: Add ¼ cup of ketchup to marinara sauce.

Make it hot: ¼ to ½ tsp ground red pepper, to marinara sauce with other ingredients when cooking.

MEATBALLS INGREDIENTS

1 lb ground beef
1 lb ground turkey or veal
1 medium onion, chopped finely
2 cloves garlic, minced
1 cup tomato sauce
2 eggs, beaten
1 tsp dried oregano
1 tsp dried basil
1 tsp dried thyme
1 tsp salt
½ tsp freshly ground pepper
½ cup breadcrumbs

DIRECTIONS

1. Preheat oven to 350F. Mix all ingredients together. (Children can help with making meatballs.)
2. Place breadcrumbs in a dish with sides at least 1" high. With your hands, roll meatballs to about 1½" in diameter. Roll each meatball in breadcrumbs. Place meatballs on parchment lined baking sheet and bake for about 20 minutes until the meatballs are firm.
3. You may freeze the meatballs at this point.
4. Add meatballs to marinara sauce and simmer over low heat for 30 minutes.
5. In the meantime, bring a pot of salted water and 1 tablespoon of olive oil to a boil and add spaghetti or pasta of choice. Follow package directions to cook al dente. Drain pasta, saving 1 cup of the pasta water. Pour desired amount of marinara sauce over pasta. Add ¼ cup of pasta water and mix, adding more if desired.
6. Place pasta and a few meatballs on every plate. If desired, grind fresh pepper over pasta.

Veggie's Bully

Let the children help with this recipe! Peeling cucumbers and avocadoes and seasoning the soup can be fun work with adult supervision.

Veggie's Bully is the second book in my Chef ReCee Jay & Friends children book series. This book features animal characters and tells the story of how Veggie Bunny feels about being bullied, her friend who wants revenge, and the voice of reason who helps them see her situation a bit differently. Bullying is not just happening in a children's playground or in school anymore. Social media has made bullying easier than ever. It's my hope that, whoever picks up this book, will remember to value how they feel about themselves, versus stressing about how others think of them.

www.amzn.to/2PkOmlw

Chilled Cucumber Soup

Serves 6

INGREDIENTS

2 tbsp vegetable oil
5 cucumbers, chopped, deseeded and peeled if not organic
3 cloves garlic, minced
2 onions, diced
2 ½ cups stock
1 avocado, peeled and seed removed
¼ cup chopped fresh dill
¼ tsp pepper

Expandthetable Suggestions:

Creamy taste: Add 1 cup cold milk just before serving. To keep the soup vegan, use a nut based milk such as almond or soy.

DIRECTIONS

1. In a large saucepan, heat the oil over medium heat and sauté the cucumbers, garlic, and onions until onions are transparent, about 6 minutes.
2. Add the broth and simmer until the cucumber is soft, about 15 minutes.
3. Remove the soup from the heat and using an immerser or placing in a blender, purée until smooth. While the mixture is still warm, stir in the dill and season with pepper.
4. Chill and serve. Garnish with some fresh dill or a thin slice of avocado

Spicier: Add 1 tbsp white horseradish before blending.

Who Knows Jordan?

Children love to help in the kitchen. Here are a few snacks that kids can make afterschool or on a weekend afternoon. Healthy and fun!

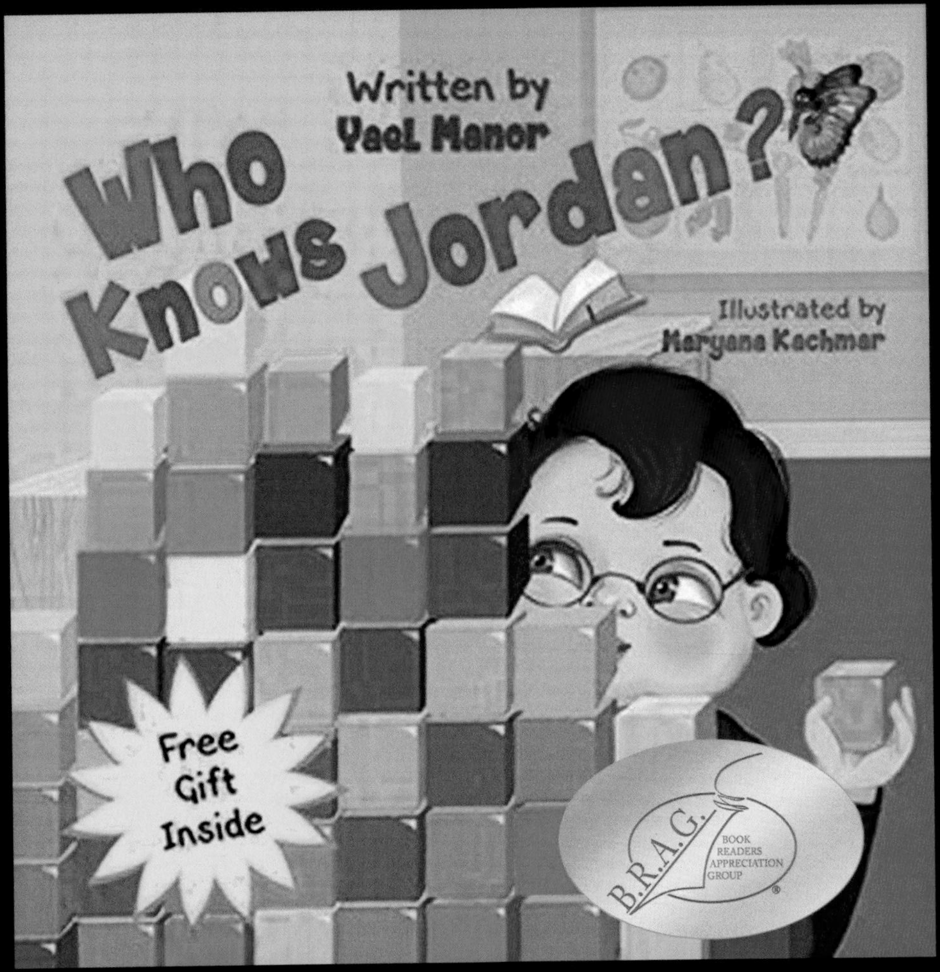

This is the story of Jordan, 5-year-old boy, who is overweight and wears glasses. Jordan is a very talented child, but it doesn't help him connect with other children. Every morning, Jordan goes to kindergarten and plays dice alone, assembles puzzles alone, plays in the yard alone and on trips, he walks alone in the back. Jordan tries to attract the attention of other children, using attention grabbers: beautiful clothes, a stylish hat, a haircut and more. One day, Larry the caterpillar appears to help Jordan. Larry helps Jordan develop self-confidence and faith in his worth as a person

www.amzn.to/32oFsXE

Ants on a Log

Serves 2

INGREDIENTS

2 stalks celery cut into 3-4″ pieces
1 apple, cut into 8ths
Nut butter, such as peanut or almond butter
Raisins

DIRECTIONS

1. Have an adult cut the celery.
2. Children can use a butter knife to spread nut butter inside the celery and on the apple.
3. Press a few raisins into nut butter.

Raw Veggies with a Dip

Serves 6

INGREDIENTS

1 carrot, cut in half and sliced into 3″ pieces
1 stalk celery, cut in half and sliced into 3″ pieces
1 bell pepper, deseeded and sliced into 3″ pieces
½ cucumber, peeled, quartered and cut into 3″ pieces
8 cherry tomatoes
5 broccoli florets
5 cauliflower florets
1 avocado
½ cup hummus
Dash of salt

DIRECTIONS

1. Have an adult cut the veggies for the children. Cut the avocado in half. Allow the children to scoop out the flesh. Mash the avocado with a fork and add a dash of salt.
2. Arrange the veggies on a plate. Put avocado and hummus in separate bowls and dip away!

FANTASY GENRE

Aerenden: The Child Returns
Meat Pies

Bulwark
Cheese Grits

Circle of Nine - Beltany
Lavender Sweet Tea Cakes

Scotland's Guardians
Simplified Haggis, Tatties 'n Neeps

Shadow Weaver
Spinach Cheese Pockets

The Outcasts
Chocolate Vampire Cupcakes

The Scribe's Daughter
Honey Rosemary Chicken

The Tempest's Roar
Vegetarian Sushi

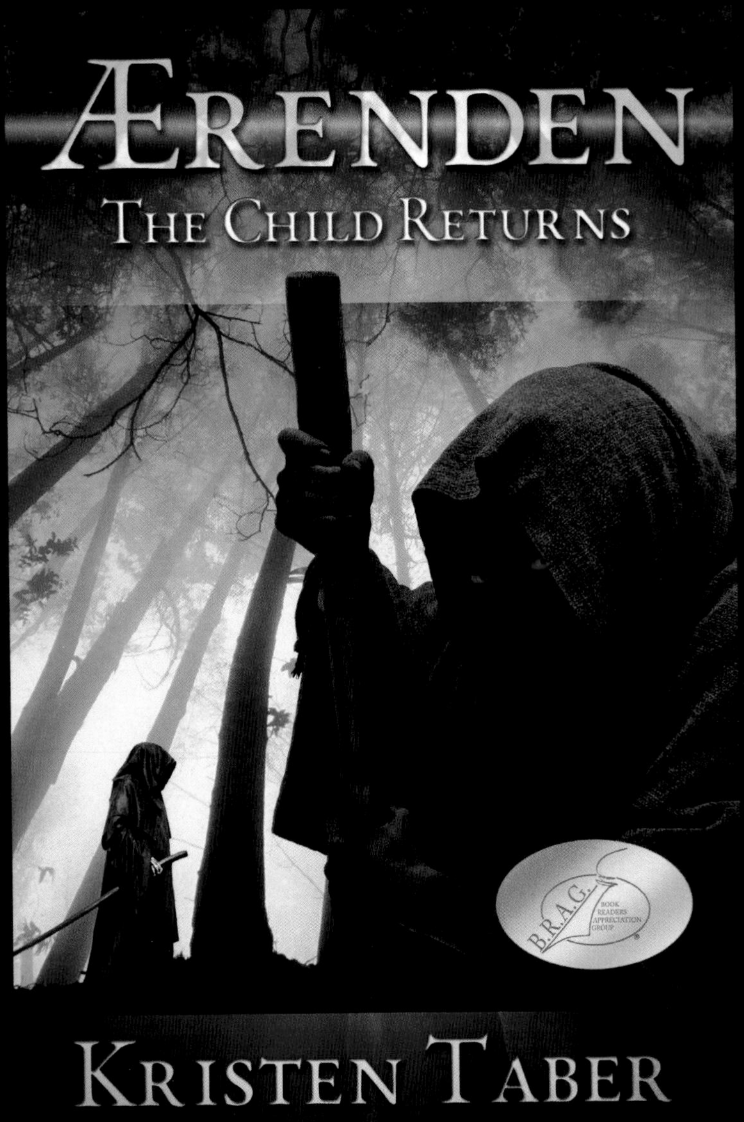

Ærenden

As Meaghan finds herself at a grand welcome feast, she would have delighted in Envelope Pies and other sweet and savory foods. Envelope pies would most certainly be served at such a grand feast! Here is our version of these tasty meat pies.

After witnessing her parents' brutal murders at the hands of red-eyed creatures, Meaghan narrowly escapes the same fate. On the run with her best friend Nick, she soon discovers that he's not from Earth and neither is she. He gives her a choice—jump through a portal into Ærenden, the war-torn kingdom of her birth, or face certain death at the hands of the creatures who hunt her. But death becomes the least of her worries when she learns that nothing in the magical land is as it appears, including Nick.

www.kristentaber.com

Meat Pie

Yields 9 pies

INGREDIENTS

2 tbsp olive oil
1 medium onion, medium dice
2 stalks celery, diced
2 cloves garlic, minced
2½ cups ground beef
½ tsp cinnamon
¼ tsp nutmeg
¼ cup potato starch dissolved in
2 tbsp water
1 cup broth
¼ cup white wine
2½ cups mixed cooked carrots, peas, mushrooms, cut into ½-inch pieces
½ cup currants or raisins
1 tsp salt
½ tsp black pepper
1 sheet puff pastry, thawed
1 egg, lightly beaten for egg wash

DIRECTIONS

1. Pre-heat oven to 375F. In a large pot, melt oil over medium heat.
2. Add onion, celery and garlic and sauté until onion is translucent, 5 minutes. Add ground beef, brown and stir in cinnamon and nutmeg.
3. Add potato starch mixture and stir constantly, about 2 minutes.
4. Add half the broth, stirring constantly, until the mixture is smooth. Add the remaining broth and wine. Bring mixture to a simmer and stir until thickened, about 5 minutes.
5. Stir in vegetables and currants. Season with salt and pepper to taste.
6. Roll pastry to ⅛-inch thickness. Cut into 9 equal pieces. Spoon 1-2 tablespoons of meat mixture into one corner of section and fold over. Press edges together with a fork, moistening the edges with water to help it stick together. Place on a parchment lined baking sheet.
7. With a sharp knife, cut 3 slits in center to allow steam to escape when baking.
8. Brush with an egg wash. Place pan in oven and bake until golden and the filling bubbles, about 15-20 minutes. Cool a few minutes before serving.

Expandthetable Suggestions:

Use ground or leftover minced chicken, lamb, bison, etc.

To make it Vegan/Vegetarian, use vegetarian stock. Add 2½ cups of cooked vegetables of choice, such as chopped zucchini, turnips, white or sweet potatoes, mushrooms, bell peppers, cauliflower, leeks, fennel, and thawed frozen peas, broccoli florets. Leftovers are great here!

Bulwark

It takes a special hand to make good grits. You must stir it slowly with deliberation. You can't rush grits. In the same way, Sheriff Clay Finnes can't rush his investigation. He has to slowly investigate, not stir the pot too hard, but just enough to keep from getting burnt.

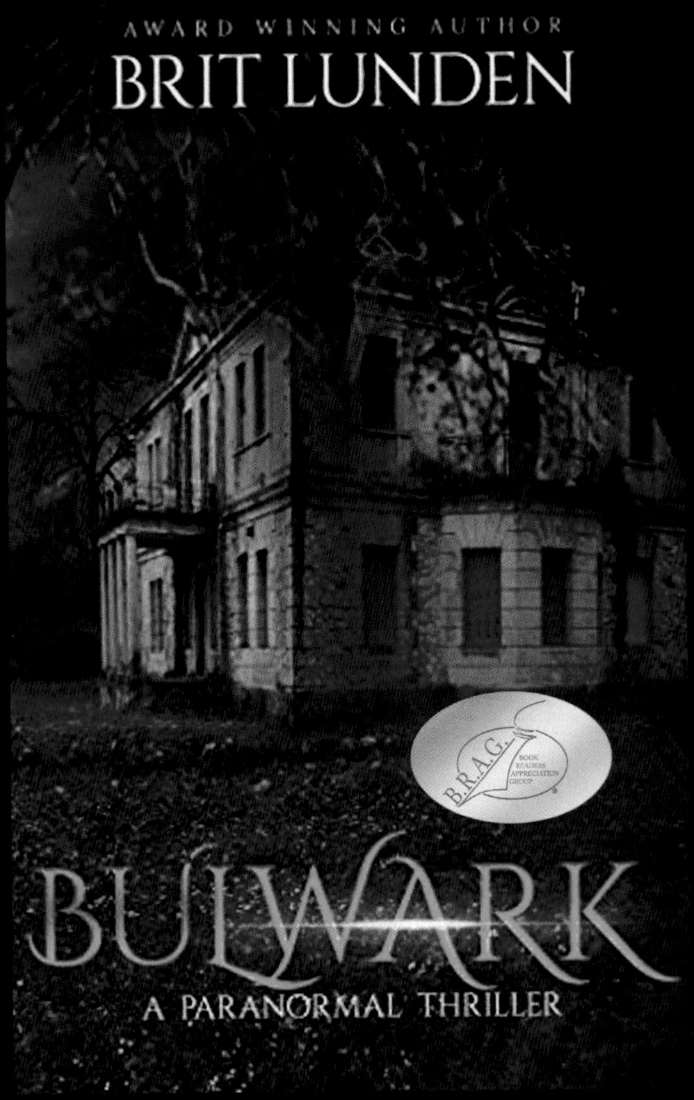

Clay Finnes is the sheriff of a small town in Georgia called Bulwark. Recently separated from his wife, all he can think about is what went wrong, and will Jenna ever come back. He's troubled by a reporter trying to build a story from what he thinks is a normal day. Clay has to admit that with the fantastical stories told by an accident victim as well as unusual sightings of wolves, things are getting a bit strange. A visit to the ominous Gingerbread House makes him realize that his life as he knows it will never be the same.

www.britlunden.com

Charlie's Mama's Grits

(Charlie is a friend of Susan Weintrob's and generously shared his Mama's perfect Grits recipe!)

Serves 4

INGREDIENTS

3 cups water
1 tsp salt
1 cup grits (not instant)
½ -1 cup milk or cream
½ cup butter
4 tsp Parmesan or grated cheddar, 1 spoonful on top of each bowl, optional.

DIRECTIONS

1. In a pot, bring water and salt to a boil. Stir grits in and continue to stir. Bring back to a boil, cover pot and lower heat to a simmer.
2. Cook for about 20 minutes, stirring from time to time. You may need to stir more vigorously as the grits thicken. Add more water if necessary.
3. Grits are done when creamy. Stir in milk or cream.

Circle of Nine - Beltany

Cooking is magic! Celeste, Brigit's mother, grows herbs and uses a lot of them in her soap making business. Brigit is not overly enthused about her mother's giant herb garden and her practice of a pagan religion, which makes them the objects of ridicule and some suspicion in their small town. Celeste is definitely a free spirit, choosing to wear long flowing gowns even in the dead of winter. This Lavender-Thyme Tea Bread is a wonderful addition to afternoon tea or for any snack or dessert. Any magic spells will have to be your own!

Brigit Quinn's 15th birthday wish is for a normal life—impossible when your mom practices a pagan religion and everyone believes she's a witch. Instead, Brigit learns she's descended from a legendary Celtic tribe that guard Ireland's ancient stone circles. A spellbound book of family history reveals powers that could be hers—if only she wanted them. When someone evil returns to steal her family's strength, Brigit must decide to defend her unique heritage or reject it for the normal life she's always craved. Teens and adults will enjoy this award-winning novel—which blends magic with Celtic mythology and pagan ritual.

www.valeriebiel.com

Lavender Tea Cake

INGREDIENTS

6 tbsp butter softened
⅓ cup honey
2 eggs, beaten
1 cup milk
1 tsp dried culinary lavender buds, chopped
1½ tsp baking powder
¼ tsp baking soda
2½ cups unbleached all-purpose flour
1 tsp fresh thyme leaves only or ½ tsp dried
1 tsp vanilla
¼ tsp salt

DIRECTIONS

1. Preheat oven to 350F. Spray a loaf pan with vegetable or butter oil.
2. Cream butter with honey. Add beaten eggs. Stir until combined.
3. Heat milk and lavender buds in a small pan over medium heat. Bring to a simmer, remove from the heat and allow to cool.
4. Mix baking powder, baking soda and flour together. Add one half at a time to egg mixture, then one half of the milk mixture. Repeat until you have used both mixtures up, mixing after each addition until combined.
5. Add thyme, vanilla and salt.
6. Add to loaf pan. Bake for 30 minutes or until a toothpick when tested in the loaf's middle comes out clean. Run a knife around the edges of the pan. Cool for 10-15 minutes and remove from pan onto a pretty plate. Time for tea!

A face without a nose watches Bryanna from a window in an Edinburgh townhouse. A Brownie! Impossible. They only exist in books. But the Brownie doesn't remain the only legendary creature she meets. Maybe I'm hallucinating. She decides to talk to her dad. However, he gets kidnapped by a woman whose scent seems surprisingly familiar to Bryanna. Without hesitation, she follows them and lands smack dab in the middle of the adventure of her life. The world she faces now is murderously dangerous. And if she survives the journey, she seems doomed to kill her father for his secret.

www.katharinagerlach.com

Scotland's Guardians

The most traditional dinner you can have in Scotland is Haggis, Tatties 'n Neeps. However, not everyone enjoys the idea of eating lamb heart, lungs and often liver cooked in a lamb's stomach. Therefore, simplified versions of the recipe exist that use more familiar ingredients but retain the flavor.

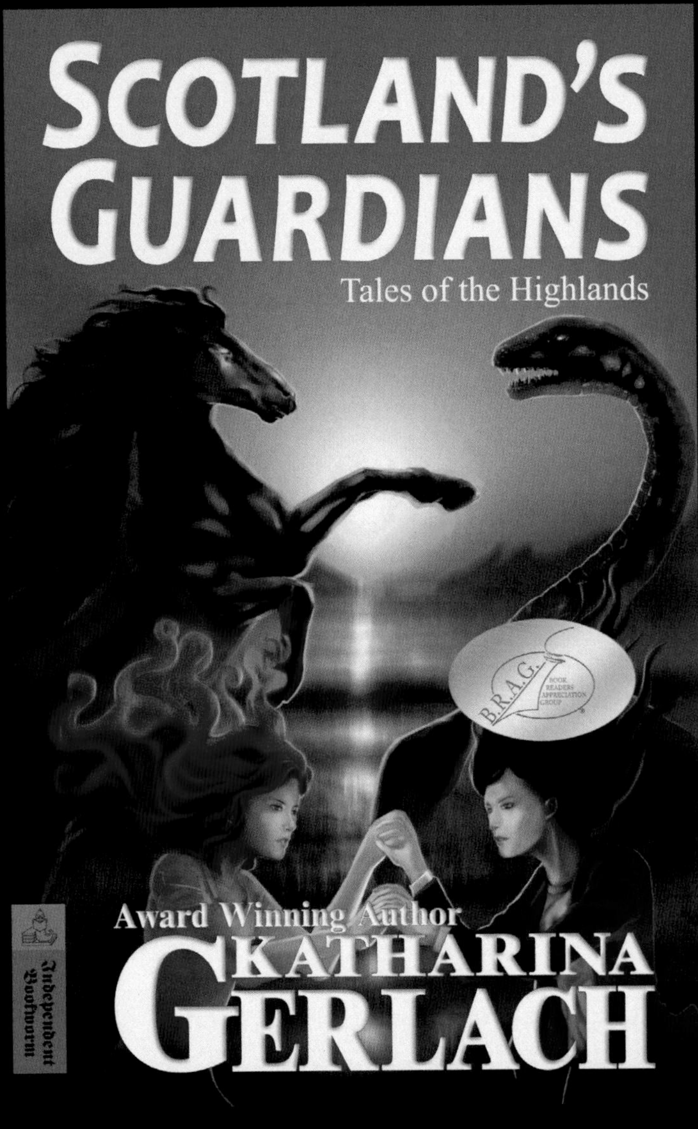

A simplified Haggis, Tatties 'n Neeps

Serves 4

INGREDIENTS

½ tbsp butter, more if needed
1 onion, diced
½ tsp ground black pepper
¾ tsp ground coriander
¾ tsp nutmeg
1 tsp allspice
½ tsp dried thyme or fresh, slightly chopped if fresh
¼ tsp cinnamon
¾ lb ground lamb (lamb mince)
½ lb chicken livers
1 cup stock
9 tbsp pinhead oatmeal (steel-cut oats)
⅔ lb potatoes
½ lb turnips or swedes (rutabagas)
5 tbsp unsalted butter
5 spring onions (can be omitted since not traditional)
4 tsp double cream
Salt, pepper, and nutmeg to taste

DIRECTIONS

1. Preheat the oven to 350F.
2. Peel and quarter the potatoes and turnips or swedes (rutabagas).
3. Warm the butter in a pan, add the onion and cook (medium heat) until softened (5 min).
4. Remove fatty or tough pieces off the chicken livers and discard. Roughly chop the rest.
5. Add the various spices and thyme to the onion, cook a minute, and then add the lamb and chicken livers.
6. Brown the meat. When it's all cooked, add the stock. Cover and simmer for 20 minutes.
7. Add the oatmeal, mix well and transfer to an oven dish. Cover the dish and put in the oven for 30 minutes.
8. Cook the turnips or swedes and the potatoes in separate pans of boiling salted water for 20 to 25 minutes until tender. Drain the vegetables and keep them separate.
9. Remove the lid from the Haggis and cook another 10 mins.
10. Return the turnips or swedes to their pan, add half the butter and mash. Keep them chunky. Season to taste (salt, pepper, a pinch of nutmeg). Cover to keep warm.
11. Trim and chop the spring onions. Melt the remaining butter in the potato pan, add the spring onions and cook for 1 to 2 minutes (until softened). Add the potatoes and mash until smooth. Season to taste (salt, pepper, a pinch of nutmeg). Cover to keep warm.
12. Take the cooked haggis from the oven and place a portion onto each warmed plate. Divide up the turnips or swedes and potatoes (neeps & tatties) and serve.

Note: US: Rutabaga; UK: Swede; Scotland: Neeps

Recipe Courtesy of Katharina Gerlach

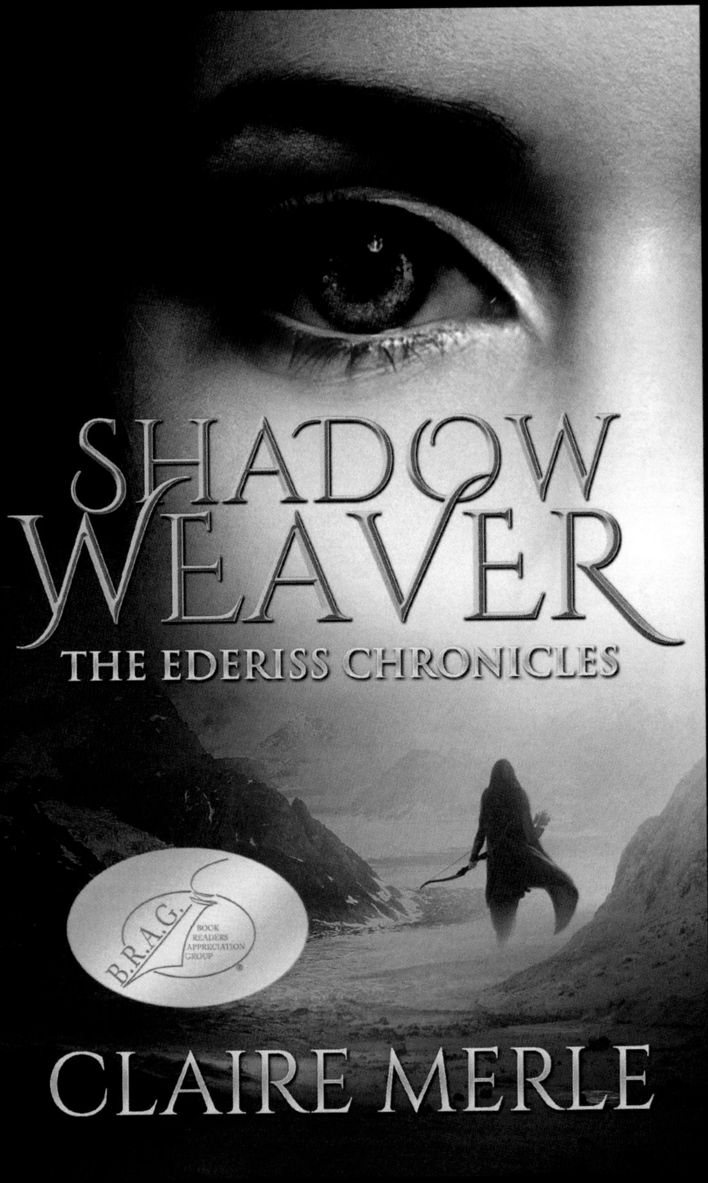

Shadow Weaver

When Mirra is imprisoned and barely fed, she is eventually served pastries with cheese, a true delight. Here is our version, without all the trauma Mira had to go through!

Sixteen-year-old Mirra can see people's memories. She is a Shadow Weaver, one of a glitter-eyed race, feared in her land and forced into slavery. She and her brother Kel have escaped their fate by hiding near the frozen mountains. But when bounty hunters snatch Kel, Mirra, injured, is forced to give herself up to stay with him. They are taken to a lawless town, Mirra is sold to the Kingdom's missing Prince, who many fear dead after an attack on his escort. The Prince needs Mirra to discover who ordered the attack, but if she fails, all hope of seeing her brother again, will be cut by the noose around her neck.

www.amzn.to/2Tcihf9

Spinach-Cheese Pockets

Yield: 9-18 pastries

INGREDIENTS

1 box frozen puff pastry, thawed (2 sheets)
2 tbsp extra virgin olive oil
1 medium yellow onion, thinly sliced
1 tsp kosher salt
½ tsp pepper
1 garlic clove, minced
1 tbsp fresh thyme leaves
¼ tsp nutmeg
8 oz frozen chopped spinach or fresh spinach steamed and squeezed dry. Chop fresh spinach if using
1½ cups shredded cheese, cheddar, Swiss or cheeses of choice. May mix.
1 egg, beaten
Sesame seeds, black and white, for garnish

DIRECTIONS

1. Remove puff pastry from freezer and defrost in refrigerator.
2. Preheat oven to 375F. Line a baking sheet with parchment paper.
3. Heat the olive oil in a large skillet over medium-high heat. Add the onions and cook 5 minutes, stirring occasionally until softened. Season with salt and pepper and continue cooking another 5-10 minutes or until the onions are golden and caramelized. Add the garlic, thyme and nutmeg, and cook another minute. Add spinach and cook until spinach is dry. Remove from the heat.
4. Stir in cheese.
5. Lay the 2 puff pastry sheets flat on parchment paper or a floured surface. Gently roll the sheets out to stretch slightly. Cut each sheet into 9 squares.
   - To make squares: Place 1 heaping spoonful of the spinach filling on 9 of the squares, leaving a ¼ inch border around the edges. Brush the edges with egg. Lay the remaining 9 squares over the filling on each of the squares and seal the edges by crimping with the tines of a fork.
   - To make triangles: Place 1 heaping teaspoon of the spinach filling towards one edge of the squares. Fold the square in half to form a triangle. Brush the edges with egg. Seal the edges by crimping with the tines of a fork.
6. Place the squares and or triangles on the parchment lined baking sheet(s) and brush the tops with beaten egg. Make 2-3 small slits on the top of the pastries. Sprinkle with sesame seeds and thyme.
7. Transfer to the oven and bake for 20-25 minutes or until golden brown.
8. Serve warm or room temperature.

Adapted from Halfbakedharvest

It's hell being a teenager, but being hunted by vampires trumps everything else as Larna Collins discovers. Mystical relics. Powerful vampires. Hunky but strange allies. Sink your teeth into this fun, fierce vampire series today!

www.mistyhayesauthor.com

The Outcasts

Larna is drawn to a seemingly quaint village, which she discovers isn't as charming as its blood-craving inhabitants want her to believe!

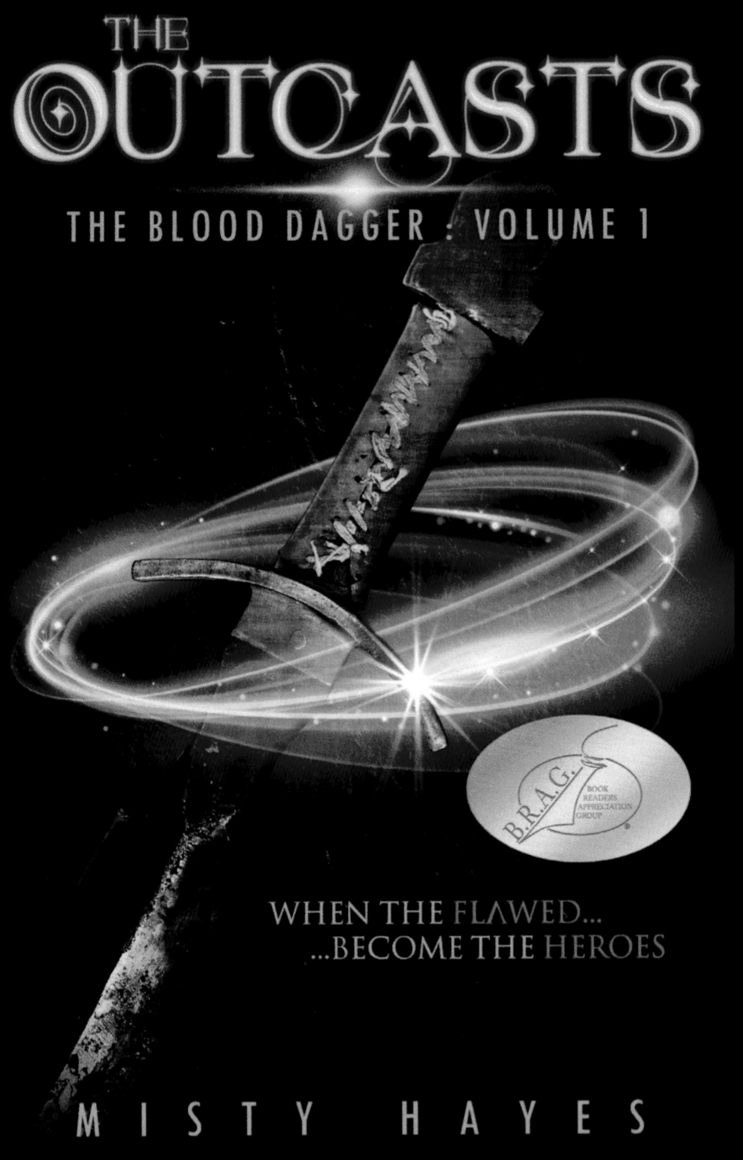

Chocolate Vampire Cup Cakes

Yield 12-14 cupcakes

CAKE INGREDIENTS

2 oz baking chocolate
½ cup butter
2 cups flour
1½ cups sugar
1 tsp baking powder
1 tsp baking soda
2 tsp espresso powder
½ tsp salt
2 eggs
1 cup cold water

DIRECTIONS

1. Preheat oven to 350F.
2. Melt chocolate and butter.
3. Mix together flour, sugar, baking powder, baking soda, espresso powder and salt. Add chocolate and butter mixture to flour mixture and stir to combine.
4. Beat eggs and water together. Add to batter and mix until smooth.
5. Place muffin papers in muffin tins and fill three quarters of the way. Bake for 20 minutes or until a toothpick comes out clean. Cool before icing.

CREAMY BUTTER ICING INGREDIENTS

2 tbsp butter
1 cup confectioner's sugar
2 tbsp milk
½ tsp vanilla

DIRECTIONS

1. Cream butter and sugar together.
2. Add milk and vanilla and mix until smooth.
3. Ice the cupcakes.
4. Warm 1 cup of seedless raspberry jam (can be sugar free) and drizzle over the cupcakes

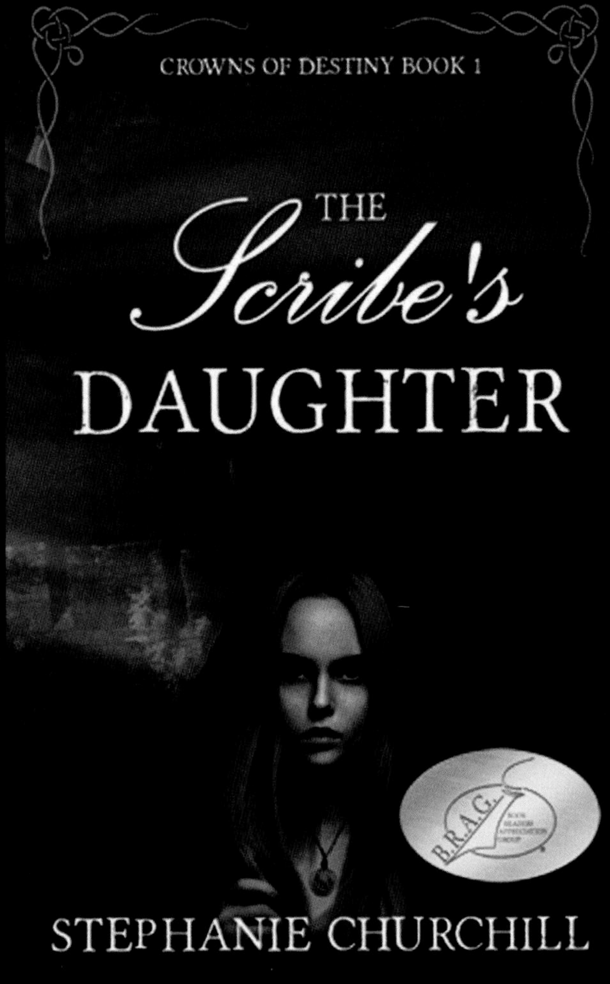

The Scribe's Daughter

As Kassia finally finds herself living in a palace, foods, such as honey, olive oil, and spices were wonderful luxuries not used by peasants. This chicken dish would be very special indeed!

As Kassia slowly unravels clues to the mysteries of her family's past, her discoveries make her a target of a man who would use her for his own dark ends. But he must catch her first.

Her only help comes from a young man who has secrets of his own. After surviving the brutalities of prison, together they flee for their lives, surviving a dark swamp, and the machinations of a strange people with disturbing customs. Clues lead them to cross the sea where finally they meet a man who has the answers. But the truth is costly.

What if everything you thought you knew was a lie?

www.stephaniechurchillauthor.com

Honey-Rosemary Chicken

INGREDIENTS

1 chicken, 3 lbs
2 tbsp olive oil
2 tbsp honey
2 tbsp vinegar
2 tbsp fresh rosemary, snipped or 2 tsp dried rosemary
2 cloves garlic, minced
Salt and pepper

DIRECTIONS

1. Preheat oven to 375F.
2. Rinse chicken, pat dry and place in oven proof pan.
3. In a bowl, mix olive oil, honey, vinegar, rosemary and garlic. Pour over chicken.
4. Bake uncovered for 1 hour until slightly browned and meat thermometer registers 160F when placed into chicken.
5. Add salt and pepper to taste.

This is a story of the whales and dolphins who rule the Seven Seas and the odyssey of a white dolphin named Apollo. If you dare to join him, Apollo will take you into a world filled with mystery and magic—a place of budding life and sudden death where the light of the sun penetrates only the upper layers, leaving the rest of its vast dominions inked in eternal darkness. When your journey is done, you will never again look the same way upon the oceans that lie beyond the thin blue line that divides his world from yours.

www.rarclouston.com

The Tempest's Roar

The world's oceans are the source of all life on earth. It is a resource we all share and depend upon, but sadly we have damaged it almost beyond repair through the ravages of pollution, global warming, and the plundering of fish stocks. It is not too late to save it and you can take one small step in that direction by replacing fish on your plate with a seaweed salad or veggie sushi.

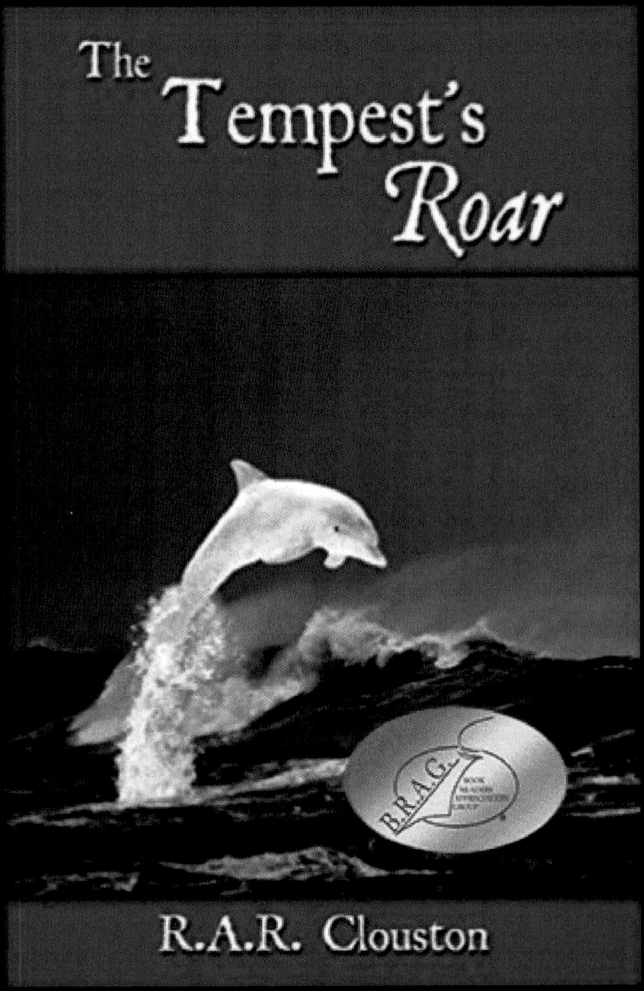

Vegetarian Sushi

RICE INGREDIENTS

½ cup of rice vinegar (white vinegar can be used)
¼ cup white sugar (reduce amount if too sweet for your taste)
1 tsp salt
2 cups water
2 cups white rice (preferably sushi rice)
4 sheets nori (edible seaweed)

DIRECTIONS

Prepare the rice:

1. Put rice and water in a saucepan with a see-through lid and bring to a boil.
2. Reduce heat to low and cook for about 20 minutes.
3. When all the water has been absorbed, let cool.
4. Mix vinegar, sugar and salt together and put in the microwave until sugar is dissolved
5. Cool and then mix into rice.
6. Stir until rice is dry – may take a bit of time.

VEGETABLES INGREDIENTS

1 red pepper
1 carrot
1 cucumber
1 avocado
1 cup of red cabbage sliced very thinly
Cut vegetables into matchsticks

DIRECTIONS TO PREPARE SUSHI ROLLS

1. Lay a layer of rice on the Nori leaving about an inch on each side and top and bottom.
2. Add a row of the vegetable you want
3. It is easiest to roll using a sushi mat, but you can use a kitchen towel.
4. When you reach the end of your roll, wet you finger and apply to nori at the end so it will seal as you finish the roll.
5. Using a very sharp knife cut into 1-inch slices.
6. Serve with dipping sauce of your choice – Soy sauce, wasabi, ginger or any of the many that are commercially available.

Historical Fiction
Genre

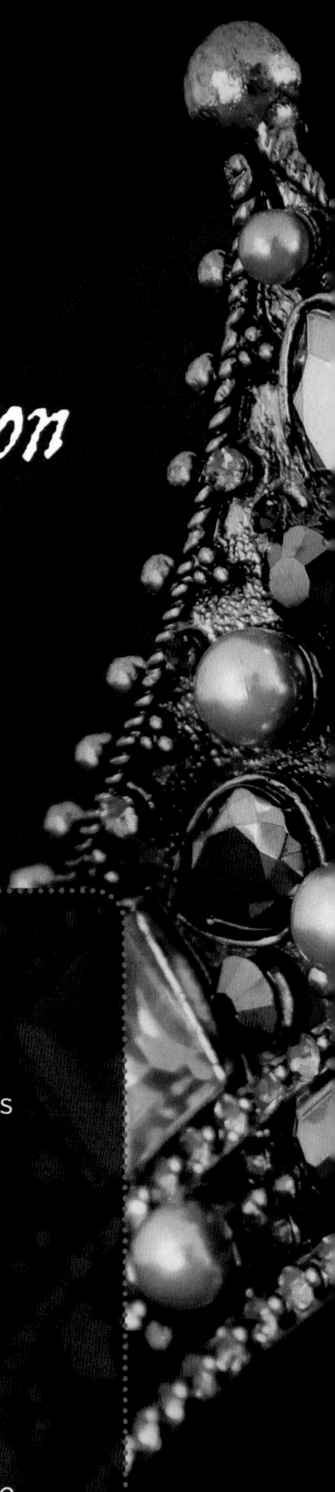

A King Under Siege
Medieval Blanc Mange

A Mistake of Consequence
Scottish Oat Scones

Acre's Orphans
Lemon Chicken Pita Pockets

Blind Tribute
Corn Bread

Blitz Pams
Panackelty

Dirt
Hearty Biscuits

Immigrant Soldier
Christmas Stollen

Imperial Passions
Mediterranean Sea Bass

Line by Line
French Bread

None of Us the Same
Newfoundland Fish Cakes

Rebels Against Tyranny
Canneloni

Sea Witch
Pirates Rum Cake

The Jøssing Affair
Gravlax

The Lady of the Tower
Roasted Potato Lyonnaise

The Plains of Chalmette
Chicken Sausage Gumbo

To Be A Queen
Rotisserie Rib Roast on grill

Richard II found himself under siege not once, but twice in his minority. He was only fourteen when the Peasants' Revolt terrorized London. But he proved himself every bit the Plantagenet successor, facing Wat Tyler and the rebels when all seemed lost. But only six years later, vengeful magnates strove to separate him from his friends and advisors and even threatened to depose him if he refused to do their bidding. The Lords Appellant, as they came to be known, murdered his closest allies, leaving the King alone and defenseless. He would never forget his humiliation and he vowed that next time, retribution would be his.

www.mercedesrochelle.com

A King Under Siege

Blanc Mange is a dish found in most every medieval cookbook. It would have been found at every royal celebration from coronations to wedding feasts.

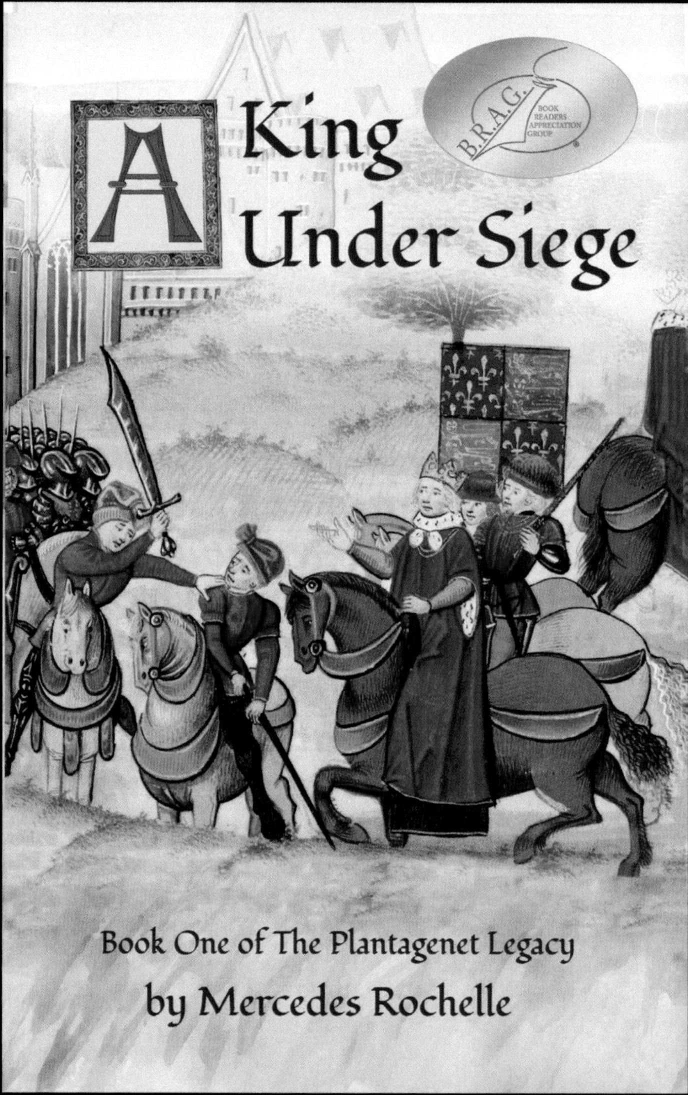

Blanc Mange Medieval Style

Serves 2-3

INGREDIENTS

1 lb chicken breast

1½ cups rice

1 cup almond milk

1 cup water

2 tsp honey

½ tsp salt

½ tsp cinnamon

¼ tsp ground ginger

¼ tsp pepper

DIRECTIONS

1. Boil chicken until soft. Cool and shred.
2. Boil rice in almond milk and water. Cook until soft, adding almond milk if rice becomes too dry.
3. Add honey, salt, ginger and pepper.
4. Add cooked chicken and stir gently.
5. Cook over medium heat until thickened. Taste and adjust seasoning

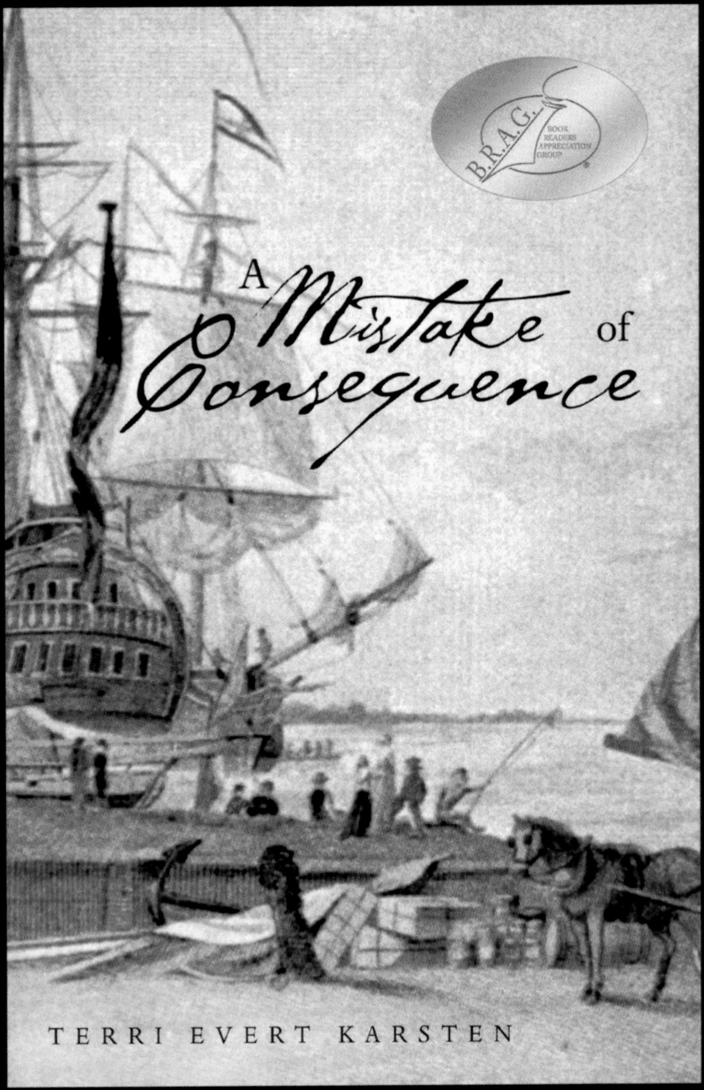

A Mistake of Consequence

All through the novel, Callie wants to return to Scotland. Surely, she would long for a taste of home. (as would Davy!) Scottish Oat Scones were first mentioned in print in the early 1500's.

1754: Following Callie Beaton's impulsive flight from yet another unwanted suitor, she is snatched from docks near Edinburgh and thrust aboard a ship to be sold as an indentured servant in the American Colonies. Two men offer her help getting home, one a handsome gentleman, the other a charming captain. But at least one of them is a murderer. Is there anyone Callie can trust? In this 18th century romantic adventure, a Scottish lass in the wrong place at the wrong time unwittingly embarks on a journey searching for love, belonging, and ultimately her true destiny.

www.terrikarsten.com

Scottish Oat Scones

Yields 10

INGREDIENTS

1½ cup flour
1½ cup uncooked rolled oats (old-fashioned, not quick)
¼ cup sugar
1 tbsp baking powder
1 tsp cream of tartar
½ tsp salt
½ cup butter, melted
½ cup milk
1 egg
½ cup currants or raisins

DIRECTIONS

1. Preheat oven to 425F. Spray baking sheet with cooking spray.
2. Combine dry ingredients. Add the butter, milk and egg. Stir in the raisins or currants.
3. Drop about ¼ cup onto greased baking sheet and flatten into about a 4 inch diameter circle. Place each round about an inch apart. Bake at 425F for 12-15 minutes.

(Adapted from Quaker Oats)

Acre's Orphans

Arabic cuisine was considered more advanced than Western cooking. The Crusaders found spices, lemons and white bread. They carried these things back to England and France to the great delight of the Royal families.

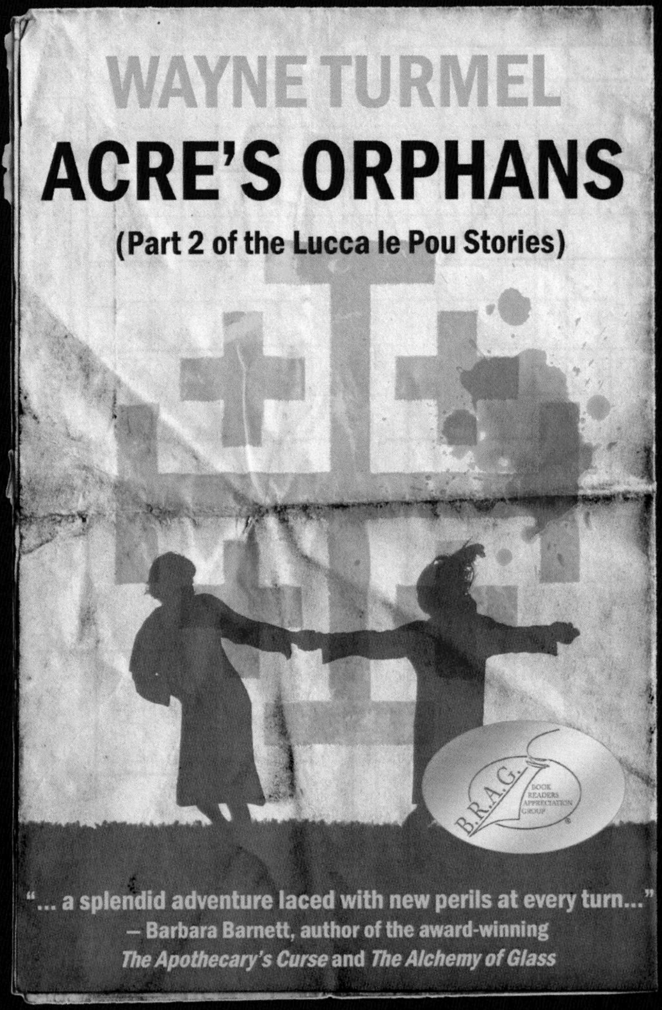

Narrowly surviving the worst disaster ever to befall the Crusaders, orphan Lucca and a young friend must now flee the doomed city of Acre. Crossing bandit-ridden countryside they face danger at every turn, and political intrigue that threatens to doom the Kingdom of Jerusalem.

www.wayneturmel.com

Lemon Chicken Pita Pockets

MARINADE INGREDIENTS

½ tsp salt
¼ tsp pepper
¼ cup olive oil
3 large cloves of garlic finely chopped
4 tbsp of lemon juice

DIRECTIONS

Mix all ingredients together and set aside

CHICKEN BREASTS INGREDIENTS

4 boneless, skinless chicken breasts.
4 pita bread pockets

DIRECTIONS

1. Pound the chicken to about ½ inch thick.
2. Put chicken breasts into a bowl and cover with marinade, cover and refrigerate overnight.
3. Put olive oil into nonstick pan large enough to place the 4 chicken breasts without crowding over medium-high heat. Cook about 5 minutes on each side until the chicken is cooked through.
4. Cut the chicken into bite size pieces.
5. Open pita pockets and add chicken and desired vegetables.
   - spinach leaves
   - cucumber
   - thinly sliced onion
   - diced tomatoes

Top with a dollop of plain yogurt if you like.
Add pine nuts for added crunch!
Squeeze a small bit of lemon onto the chicken and vegetables if desired
Garnish with a wedge of lemon.

Political parties manipulate the public and the media, grasping for votes and consolidating power. Foreign nations peddle influence to achieve their own ends. The struggle between citizens and government tugs at the threads of the American Constitution and democracy itself. In a matter of moments, the United States will shatter, beginning the long march of the American Civil War. Harry Wentworth, gentleman of distinction and journalist of renown, Executive Editor of the Philadelphia Daily Standard, tries to arrest the momentum of both Union and Confederacy. To his sorrow and disgust, his calls for peaceful resolution fall on deaf ears

www.mariannechristie.com

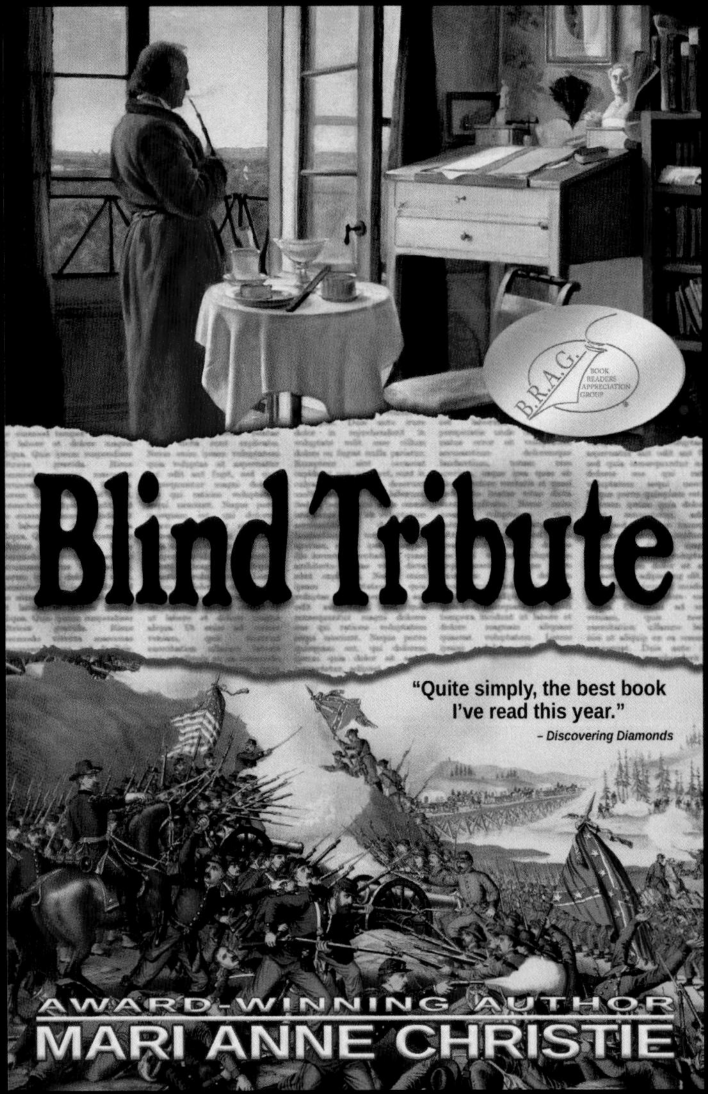

Blind Tribute

"A knock at the door revealed Elsbeth with cold drinks and glasses, followed by Maisie and Tobias carrying his requested foodstuffs, along with a cast-iron skillet, a salt cellar and pepper mill, and a basket of cornbread and pan of cobbler."

From *Blind Tribute*

Corn Bread

INGREDIENTS

1 cup yellow corn meal
1 cup white flour, sifted
3 tbsp sugar
4 tsp baking powder
½ tsp salt
1 egg
1¼ cups buttermilk
¼ cup melted butter
½ cup fresh corn kernels or frozen corn, defrosted

DIRECTIONS

1. Sift dry ingredients together.
2. Add egg, buttermilk, melted butter and beat until batter is smooth.
3. Mix in corn.
4. Pour into a greased 8-inch pan.
5. Bake at 425F for 25 to 30 minutes, until top is golden brown.

Recipe courtesy of Mari Anne Christie

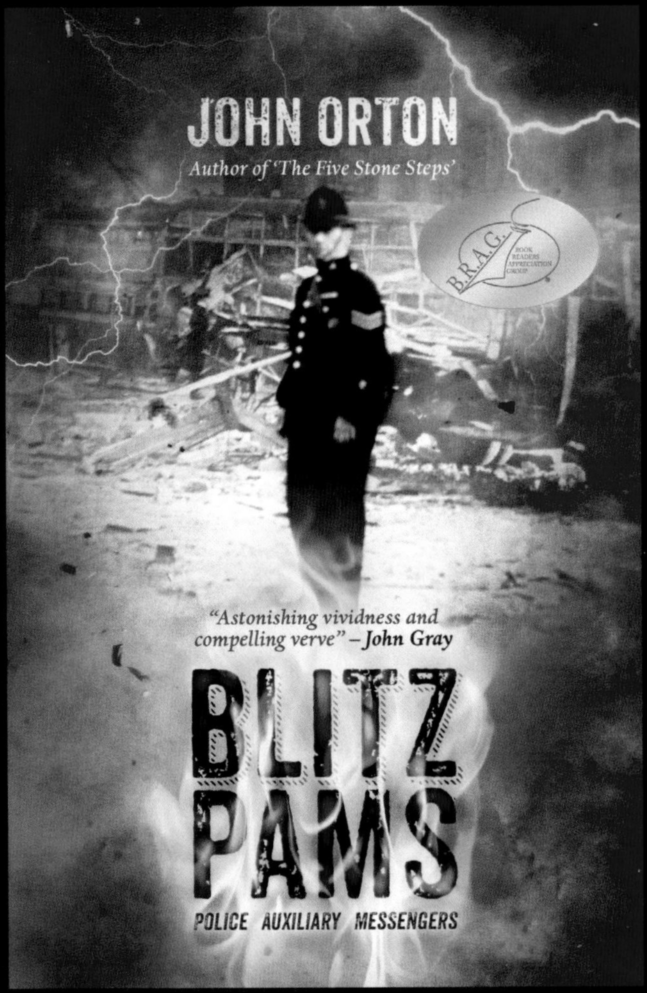

Blitz Pams

During the Second World War when nearly everything was rationed, and certain foods were never seen, neighbours gathered canned foods, and Mossie's Mam cooked and shared Panackelty and tea.

In September 1940 the German blitzkrieg over South Shields, England, had just started, with worse to come. The Police need more young PAMs (Police Auxiliary Messengers) to be ready to take messages on their bikes in the event of a raid and if the phone lines are down. Mossie Hamed, grocery delivery boy, is one of the volunteers who become the Blitz PAMs. Although, in his own words 'not over clever', Mossie tells how the next eighteen months change the lives of him and his 'marras' (mates) and of the many other unsung heroes on the home front.

https://amzn.to/2TrPaWz

Panackelty

Serves 3-4

INGREDIENTS

1 tin of corned beef, sliced
3-4 large potatoes, peeled and sliced
1 large onion, sliced
2 rashers of bacon, sliced (about 3 slices per rasher)
2 large carrots, peeled and sliced
2 tbsp butter or oil
¾ pint of stock
Dash of Worcestershire Sauce
2 oz cheddar, optional garnish

DIRECTIONS

1. Preheat oven to 350F.
2. Sauté onions in butter or oil over a medium heat. Add slices of bacon.
3. Layer onions, carrots, potatoes, corned beef or bacon in an oven proof casserole dish. Finish with a layer of potatoes on top.
4. Add a dash of Worcestershire Sauce to the stock. Pour the stock mixture over the layers. Cover.
5. Bake for 45 minutes. Remove cover to see if potatoes are soft. If so, dot butter over potatoes. If the stock has evaporated, add a bit more. Return casserole dish to oven and bake for another 15-20 minutes or until the potatoes are browned.
6. Garnish with cheddar if desired and serve with crusty bread and fresh green vegetables.

Recipe Courtesy of John Orton

Dirt

Biscuits really are a big part of this story since they represent to Sammy one of the losses that were just out of reach but not gone forever. A memory of his mother.

When thirteen-year-old Sammy wakes and finds he and his seven-year-old sister, Birdie, are now orphans, he vows never to go to the state home. Holding on to the pretense that their parents are still alive, Sammy and Birdie learn the art of lying and the terrible burden it carries. A mangy stray dog and a cantankerous old woman become the lifeline the children need to survive and brings Sammy to the realization that a good heart is sometimes disguised.

Mother Nature, the Great Depression, and the Dust Bowl all contrive to weed out the weakest. But Sammy discovers a strength he never knew he owned along with a mighty big dose of fear.

http://sharond1.sg-host.com/index.html

Old Fashioned Biscuits

Yields 12 biscuits

INGREDIENTS

2 cups unbleached flour
2 tbsp baking powder
1 tbsp sugar
1 tsp salt
4 tbsp butter
¾ cup milk
2 tbsp butter for brushing tops

DIRECTIONS

1. Preheat oven to 400F.
2. Mix flour, baking powder, sugar and salt.
3. Cut in butter with pastry cutter. Stir milk in gradually until soft dough is formed.
4. Turn out on slightly floured board and lightly knead to shape.
5. Roll ½ inch thick and cut with 2 inch floured biscuit cutter.
6. Bake on parchment covered cookie sheet in a 400F oven for 12-15 minutes.

Immigrant Soldier

Stollen is thought to have originated in 1329. It is a traditional Christmas treat in Germany. This tasty fruit cake was a tradition in Herman's family (the hero of Immigrant Soldier).

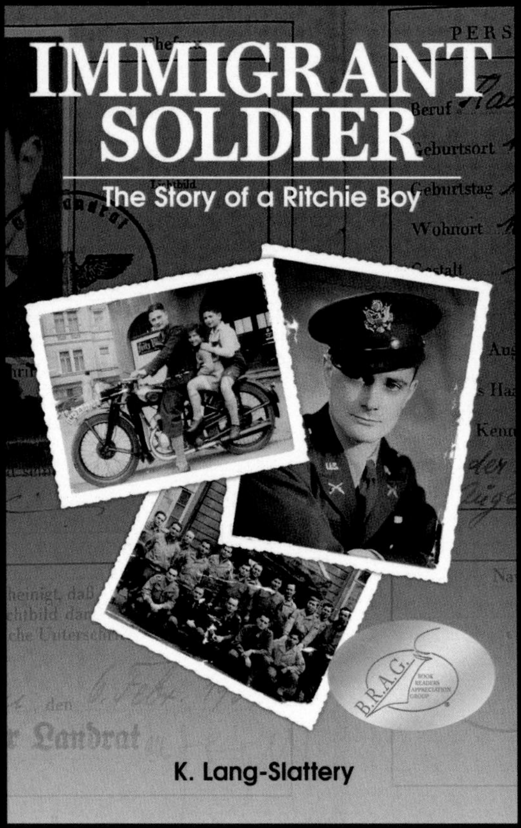

Immigrant Soldier, based on the true experiences of a refugee from Nazi Germany, combines a coming-of-age story with an immigrant tale and a World War II adventure. On a November morning in 1938, Herman finally realizes that, as a Jew, he must flee Germany, a decision that catapults him from one adventure to another, his life changed forever. Herman experiences fear, romance, horror and compassion as he evolves from a frustrated teenager, looking for a place to belong, into a confident US Army intelligence officer who struggles with hate and forgiveness.

www.klangslattery.com

Lang Family Christmas Stollen (two loaves)

INGREDIENTS

1 cup whole milk, lukewarm (105 to 110F.)
3 tbsp active dry yeast (this is slightly more than one packet)
½ cup sugar
4 cups all-purpose flour
1 large egg plus 2 egg yolks
¾ cup (1 & ½ sticks) unsalted butter, at soft room temperature
2 tsp pure vanilla extract
½ tsp almond extract
zest of 1 lemon
1 tsp salt
¾ tsp ground cardamom
¾ tsp ground nutmeg
½ tsp cinnamon
3 cups of an assortment of dried fruit, chopped. Candied citron is traditional, but a mixture could include dark raisins, pale raisins, currants, chopped apricots, chopped dried cherries, dried cranberries, dried maraschino cherries, and candied pineapple.
⅓ cup rum (dark preferable but light is ok)
½ cup chopped or slivered blanched almonds.

For Glaze:

1 stick melted butter
powdered sugar

DIRECTIONS

1. Place all dried fruit in bowl and pour the rum over the mixture. Let sit at least 1 hour or overnight.
2. Heat the milk in a glass bowl in the microwave until just lukewarm (105 to 110F.)
3. Gently stir yeast plus 2 tablespoons of the sugar into the milk. Let sit for about 10 to 15 minutes until very frothy.
4. In large bowl, place flour, rest of sugar, egg and egg yolks, very soft butter, vanilla and almond extract, lemon zest, salt, spices (cardamom, nutmeg and cinnamon) and mix with large spoon.
5. Add milk and yeast mixture and mix gently to moisten the flour. Knead the dough by hand or with a dough hook mixer for about 8 minutes until dough is smooth and elastic.
6. Scoop out of bowl, cleaning sides well. Lightly coat sides of bowl with oil and return dough to oiled bowl. Turn dough once to coat it with oil too. The dough ball should now be smooth and roundish. Cover loosely with plastic wrap or a clean kitchen cloth and put it in warm place without a draft. A slightly heated oven turned off is fine. Let rise for at least an hour until double in size.
7. Punch the dough down. Pour off any unabsorbed rum from the fruit mixture. Add dried fruit mixture and almonds to the dough. Knead into the dough by hand or with dough hook mixer.
8. Turn the dough onto a floured board and cut it into two equal halves. Press and roll each section into large, flat, oval about 1 inch thick. Fold lengthwise, one third of dough toward and just beyond center. Fold the other side over so it overlaps the first. The edge of the dough should be just past the center of the loaf thus created.
9. Placed formed dough loaves on parchment lined baking sheet large enough so they don't touch. Cover loosely with plastic wrap or clean kitchen towel and place in warm, draft free spot or into slightly warmed oven. Allow to rise for 45 to 60 minutes.
10. Preheat oven to 350F. Carefully pick out any fruit that is sticking out of the loaf (it can burn during baking.)
11. Bake the stollen for 30 to 40 minutes until golden.
12. Remove from oven and let sit 5 minutes. Use toothpick or wooden skewer to poke holes in top of crust. Brush liberally with melted butter. Dust loaves liberally with powdered sugar. Rub sugar into creases.
13. Let sit until it cools completely. Can be eaten at this point.
14. To store, wrap in plastic wrap or foil and leave to ripen in a cool place for up to 2 weeks. Or the loaves can be frozen.

Recipe Courtesy of Kathryn Slattery

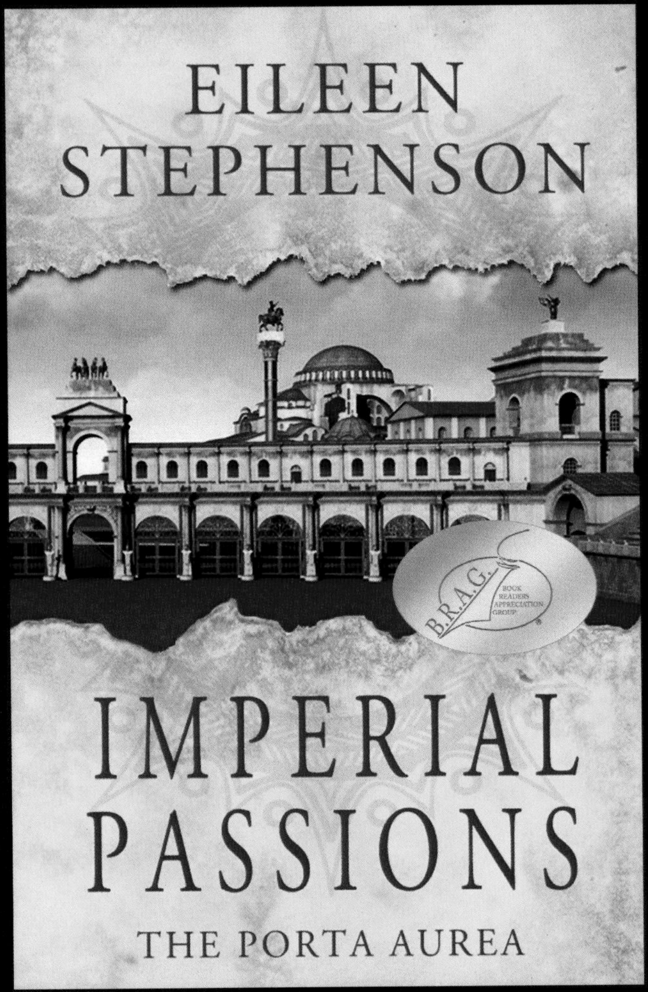

Imperial Passions

Constantinople was a city of fine dining, and fish was the main source of protein. The wealthy believed fish caught in large quantities like mackerel, anchovies or sardines were for the poorer inhabitants. They preferred big white fleshed fish like sea bass. These fish were common in the waters surrounding Constantinople during the Byzantine era and would have been served in the Great Palace to Anna Dalassena and her family

At the center of Byzantine society, orphaned Anna Dalassena lives with her grandparents among the most powerful men and women in Constantinople. The cutthroat imperial politics of the Great Palace sends the family into exile in a distant corner of the empire. Her bleak situation finally turns promising after meeting the handsome young soldier, John Comnenus before they are finally permitted to return home. Power struggles, uprisings, betrayals at the highest levels of the empire push Anna and John unwillingly into its center. When rebellion puts everyone's lives at risk, is the reward – a throne for her family – too big a gamble?

www.eileenstephenson.com

Mediterranean Grilled Fish

INGREDIENTS

1½ lbs fish, such as sea bass or salmon
kosher salt and pepper
1½ tbsp oregano
½ tsp paprika
1-2 garlic cloves, minced
juice of 1 lemon

DIRECTIONS

1. Pat fish dry on both sides. Mix together salt, pepper, oregano and paprika. Mix in garlic and lemon. Rub mixture on both sides of the fish.
2. Heat up grill. Place fish on oiled grill in an oiled basket made for fish or on a grilling tray.
3. Grill fish for about 4-5 minutes on each side or until fish is opaque all the way through.
4. Remove to a warm plate. Squeeze lemon on fish. Serve on top of rice and toasted almonds.

The 1930s: As the Great Depression deepens and her family disintegrates, Maddy Skobel flees her central Ohio town —by freight train—determined to make her own way. Learning to survive as a hobo while facing hardship, danger, and violence, Maddy must discover her own resourcefulness and strengths. Through Maddy's eyes, Line by Line explores larger themes that still resonate today: coming of age in times of economic devastation, trust in our government, and the life-shaping influence of family—both the family that we are born into and the family we create as we surround ourselves with those who matter most.

www.writersuncorked.wordpress.com

Line by Line

Working for a bakery that featured wonderful breads was a central part of Maddy's life. Wonderful fresh baguettes would have been a great treat.

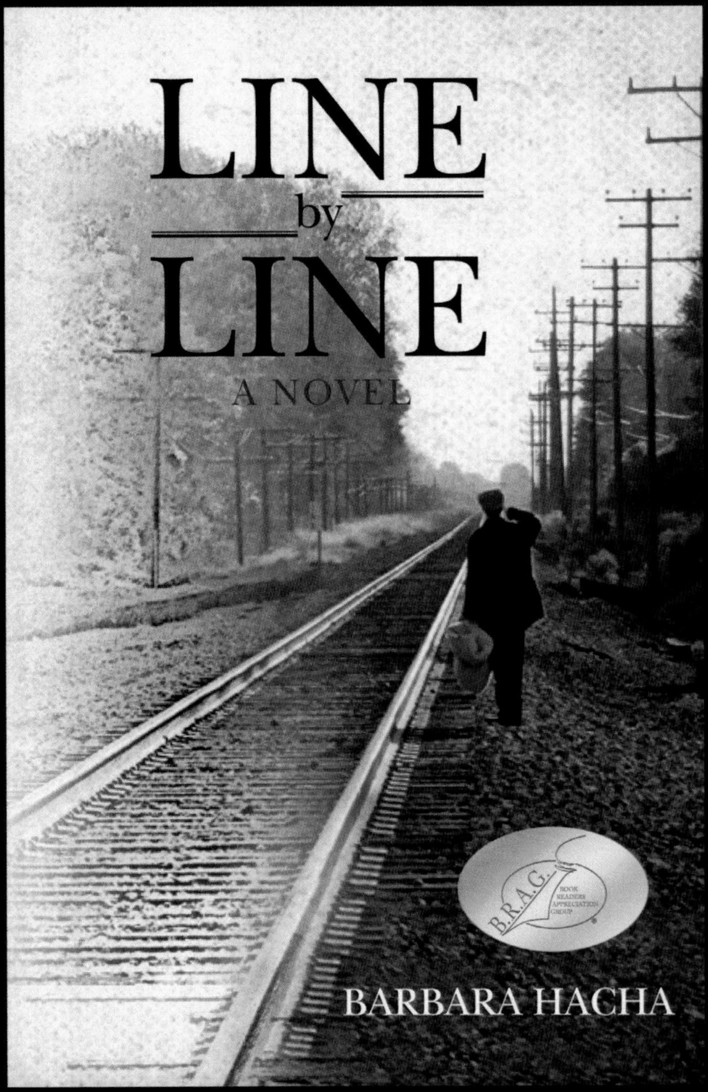

French Bread

Yield 2 medium loaves

INGREDIENTS

1 package yeast
1½ cups warm water
1 cup gluten or bread flour
3 cups all-purpose flour.
1 tbsp sugar
2 tsp salt
2 tbsp oil to coat bread
1 egg white with 1 tsp cold water

DIRECTIONS

1. Dissolve yeast in the warm water. Stir gently and wait for yeast to bubble slightly.
2. Add salt and sugar. Blend in 1 cup of gluten flour. Add enough all-purpose flour to make a sticky dough.
3. Turn out onto a lightly floured surface and knead, adding flour as dough becomes sticky. Knead until dough is smooth and elastic.
4. Add the oil to the bowl. Place the dough back in the bowl, turning once to coat. Cover with a cloth or plastic wrap and place in a draft free location. Let rise until doubled, about 1 hour. Punch down until the dough is deflated and turn back out onto the floured surface. Knead for a few moments, then divide dough into 2 pieces and shape into baguettes, pinching ends together with your fingers. Dip your fingers in room temperature water if dough doesn't stick together. Cover the dough and let rise about 40-50 minutes. Preheat oven to 400F.
5. After dough has risen, with a sharp knife, slice 2-3 diagonal lines into the dough, about ¼" deep. Brush with egg white mixture.
6. On the bottom of the oven, place a pan of water in an oven proof pan. Place loaves on a cornmeal dusted pan or on parchment lined pan.
7. Bake the loaves on a rack in the middle of the oven until crusty and golden brown, about 50-55 minutes. With a water sprayer, spray oven with a few spritzes of water midway through the baking. This helps make the crust nice and crusty. If bread appears pale, bake another 5 minutes. The bottom of the loaf should sound hollow when gently wrapped with your knuckles.
8. Remove from oven and cool on wire rack. Wrap in a cloth to keep fresh—best not to refrigerate. Bread will last 2-3 days.
9. To freeze: Bring loaves to room temperature. Wrap each loaf in plastic wrap and then aluminum foil, making sure all the surfaces of the bread are covered. Freeze for up to 3 months.
10. To make rolls: Follow recipe until you divide the dough into 2 pieces. Divide each piece into 8-9 pieces. Make into little baguette shapes, tie in a knot or shape into little round loaves. Let rise until double. Slash once down the center. Place on parchment lined baking pan. Bake for 12-15 minutes until light brown.

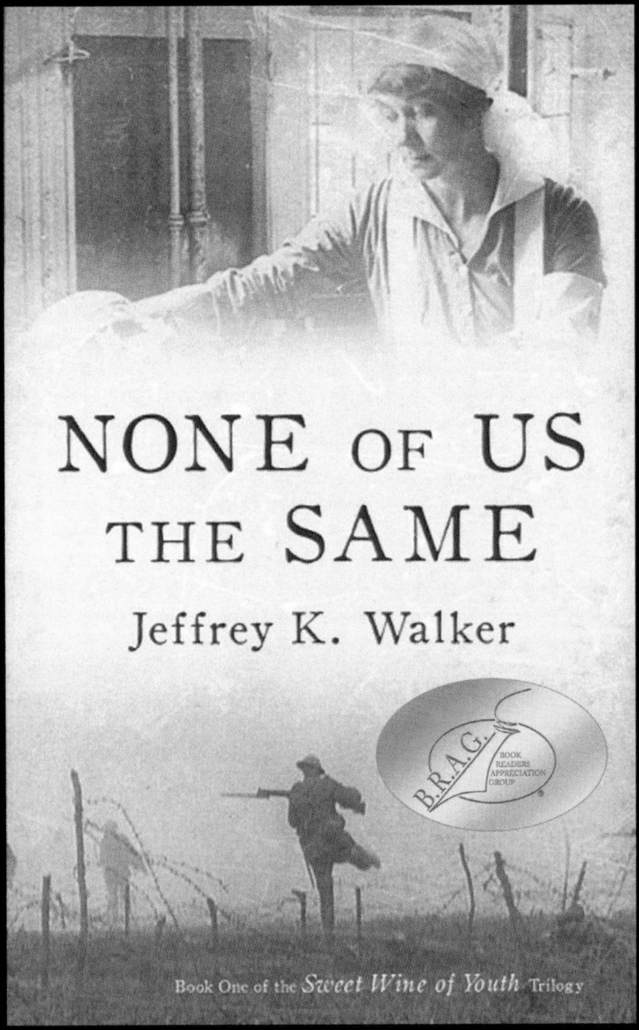

None of Us the Same

For hundreds of years, cod has been a critical resource to the people of Newfoundland and fish cakes are a staple on many a kitchen table.

Irish nurse Deirdre Brannigan has decided opinions on most things. She certainly hates the very idea of war in 1914, but she nevertheless lands in the fray where she soon unravels. Newfoundland pals Jack and Will think the war a grand adventure. After all, it couldn't possibly last long. They learn quickly how wrong they are, battered by the carnage in France. Amidst unspeakable agonies, the bloody war brings the three together. As their lives intertwine, somehow survival seems possible and a sliver of hope, love and redemption emerges.

www.jeffreykwalker.com

Newfoundland Fish Cakes

Yield 12-14 cakes

INGREDIENTS

1 lb cod
1 egg, beaten
1 small onion, finely chopped
½ tsp salt
¼ tsp pepper
¼ tsp thyme
1 tsp dill
2 cups mashed potatoes, about 3 medium potatoes
¼ cup butter

DIRECTIONS

1. Preheat oven to 350F. Poach cod in water that covers it in an oven proof pan with sides of at least 2 inches. Simmer for 12-15 minutes or until the fish flakes easily with a fork. Carefully remove from oven, drain and let cool.
2. Flake fish and add egg, onion, salt, pepper, thyme and dill. Mix to combine. Add mashed potato and mix well.
3. Use an ice cream scoop for measuring amount of fish mixture. Form mixture into cakes.
4. Melt butter in large skillet over medium heat. Place fish cakes in skillet and fry on both sides until golden. Turn only once.
5. Place fish cakes on paper towels as you finish frying them. Serve alone or with Cucumber Dill Sauce.

Cucumber Dill Sauce

This is a sauce that is great on almost any fish. In fact, can't think of any fish the sauce doesn't go with!

2 tbsp onions, minced
½ English cucumber, minced
1 tsp white horseradish
1 tbsp fresh lemon juice
½ cup mayonnaise
1 tbsp dill

Mix together. Lasts in refrigerator for 7-10 days.

Expandthetable suggestions:

Poaching liquid: If you wish, add 1 tsp salt, 2 tbsp chopped onion, 1 celery stalk sliced, and one carrot chopped.

Emperor Frederick II, called "enlightened" by historians yet decried as a despot by contemporaries, unleashes a civil war that tears the Holy Land apart. The heir to an intimidating legacy, a woman artist, and a boy king are caught up in the game of emperors and popes. Set against the backdrop of the Sixth Crusade, Rebels against Tyranny takes you from the harems of Sicily to the Holy Sepulcher in Jerusalem, from the palaces of privilege to the dungeons of despair. This is a timeless tale of youthful audacity taking on tyranny—but sometimes courage is not enough...

www.helenapschrader.com

Rebels Against Tyranny

Sicily is the oldest Italian and Western location on record where pasta was used, dating back to the 12th century. Frederick II would certainly have enjoyed this new (to him!) and delightful dish.

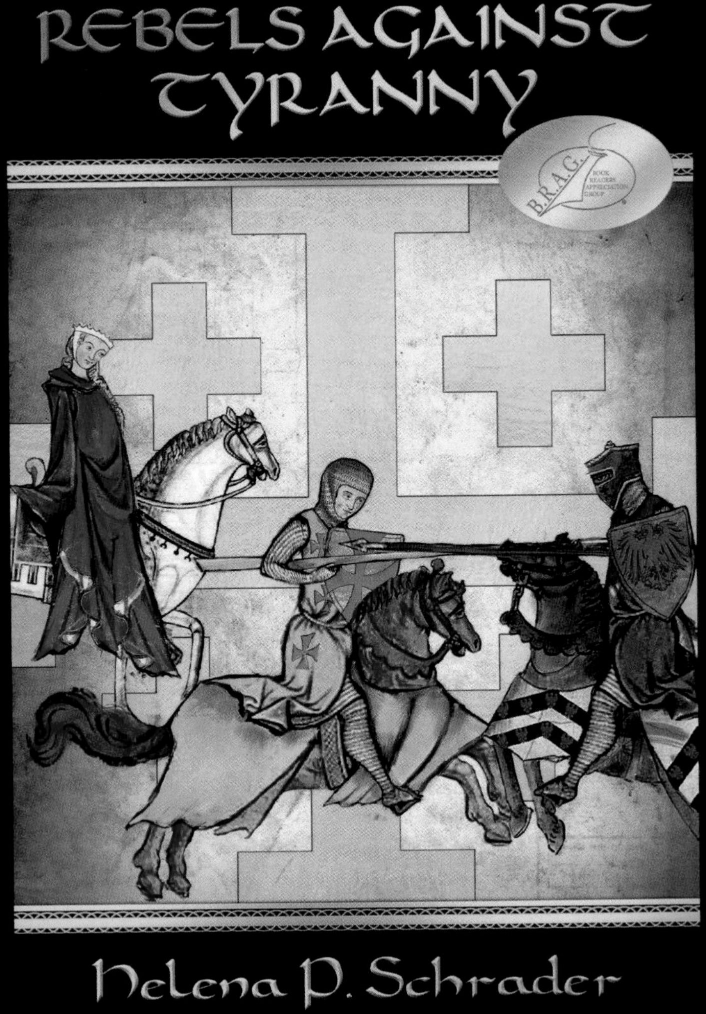

Cannelloni

FILLING INGREDIENTS

2 tbsp olive oil
¼ cup chopped onion
1 tsp finely chopped garlic
1 10 oz. pkg. chopped spinach (defrosted)
2 tbsp butter
2 eggs
1 lb. ground beef
5 tbsp heavy cream
¼ tsp each: oregano, salt, pepper
1 cup grated Parmesan cheese

DIRECTIONS

1. Cook onions & garlic in oil, add spinach & cook gently till all moisture evaporates. Put in a mixing bowl.
2. Melt butter in pan, lightly cook meat.
3. Add to mixture & add cheese, cream, eggs, spices.

Tomato Sauce: 3 cups of bottled sauce of choice.

BECHAMEL SAUCE (WHITE SAUCE) INGREDIENTS

4 tbsp butter
4 tbsp flour
1 cup milk
1 tsp salt
1 cup heavy cream

DIRECTIONS

1. Melt butter and mix in flour well (don't brown).
2. Remove from the heat and add milk and cream.
3. Stirring well.
4. Heat until thick & smooth.
5. Add salt and set aside.

Large Pasta Shells: boil in salted water until tender (not too soft or they will fall apart).

ASSEMBLING

1. Fill cooked & drained shells with the spinach-meat mixture.
2. In a 9 by13 inch pan, put a layer of tomato sauce, place shells on top, cover with the white sauce, put remaining tomato sauce on top.
3. Sprinkle with grated cheese, dot with butter.
4. Bake: uncovered at 375F for 20 minutes- until bubbling.
5. Put under the low broiler for just a few minutes to brown the top after cooking.

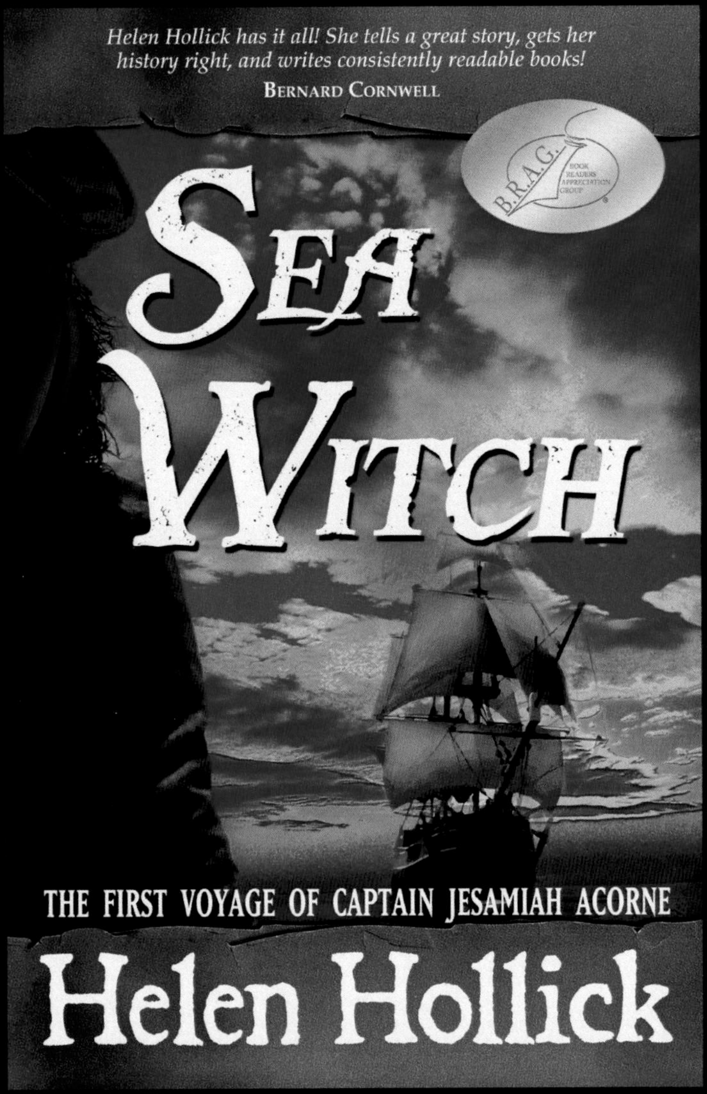
Helen Hollick has it all! She tells a great story, gets her history right, and writes consistently readable books!
Bernard Cornwell
B.R.A.G.
Sea Witch
The First Voyage of Captain Jesamiah Acorne
Helen Hollick

Sea Witch

"The mosquitoes were a nuisance, they always were, wherever you went. Jesamiah as with many a sailor, nursed a theory that drinking rum kept them away."

From *Sea Witch*

Escaping bullying by his elder half-brother, from the age of fifteen Jesamiah Acorne has been a pirate with only two loves - his ship and his freedom. But life is changed when he meets Tiola an insignificant girl, or so he assumes - until she rescues him from pirate hunters and he discovers what she really is; a healer, a midwife - and a white witch. Tiola and Jesamiah become lovers, but when the call of the sea and an opportunity to commandeer a beautiful ship - the Sea Witch - is put in Jesamiah's path he must choose between his love for the sea or for Tiola...

www.helenhollick.net

Pirates Rum Cake

INGREDIENTS

Cake

2 cups flour
⅓ cup cornstarch
1½ cups sugar or ¾ cup Stevia
2 tsp baking powder
1 tsp salt
5 eggs
½ cup vegetable oil
½ cup milk of choice (cow, almond or soy)
1 tsp lemon juice
½ cup rum
2 tsp vanilla

Rum Butter Sauce

½ cup unsalted butter or dairy free margarine
¼ cup water
½ cup sugar or ¼ cup Stevia
½ cup rum
1 tsp vanilla

DIRECTIONS

1. Spray the Bundt cake pan with oil and dust cake pan with flour to prevent sticking.
2. Combine dry ingredients in a bowl.
3. In a separate bowl, mix eggs with oil, milk of choice, lemon juice, rum and vanilla extract. Add half of liquid to dry ingredients and mix until smooth. Add rest of liquid, beating until smooth.
4. Pour the batter into prepared pan and bake in 350F oven for about 20 minutes. Lower the temperature to 300F and bake for another 20 minutes. Test cakes with a toothpick to see if done.

RUM BUTTER SAUCE:

1. In a small saucepan, cook rum butter sauce ingredients over medium heat, stirring, until sugar dissolves.
2. Allow cake to cool. Then using a toothpick to poke holes in the cake, gradually pour half of the rum sauce over the cake. Let the cake rest until the sauce is absorbed.
3. Turn the cake out onto a serving plate and pour the remaining sauce over the cake.
4. Serve and enjoy with choruses of "Ho, ho, ho and a bottle of rum!"

The Jøssing Affair

"The hotel was a large two-story building commanding an excellent view of the fjord and its high walls looking out to its mouth. It had a comfortable sitting room as well as a dining room that boasted a fine gravlaks—dish salmon cured in brandy and fresh dill — and several other similar delicacies from the sea when in season."

From *The Jøssing Affair*

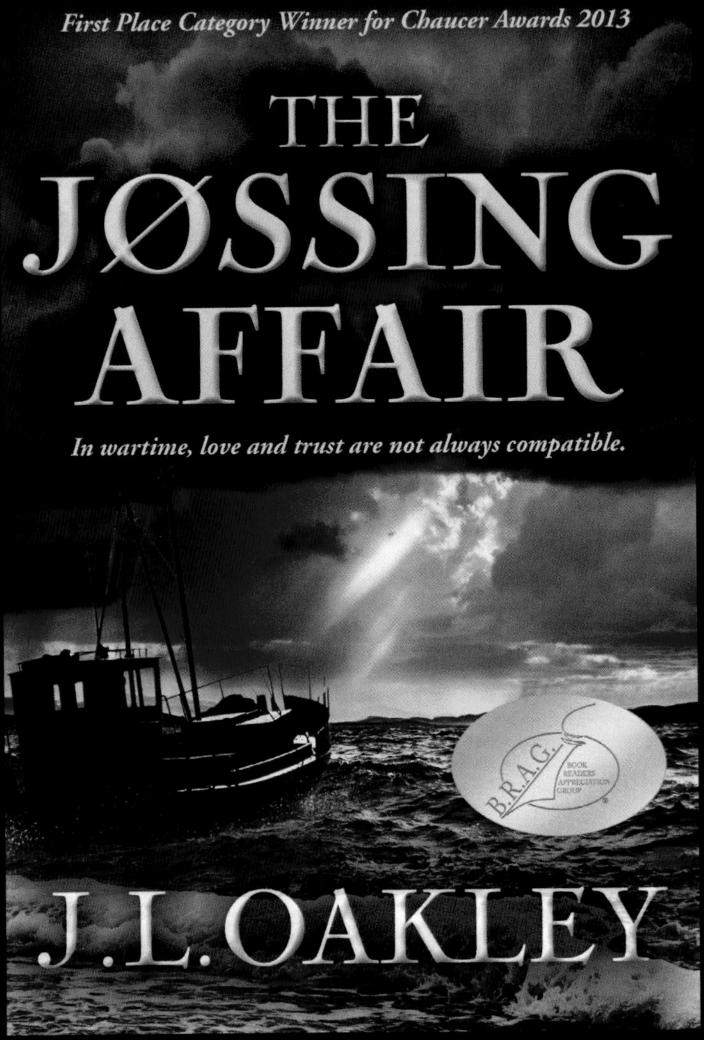

An intelligence agent, posing as a deaf fisherman, delivers arms and agents to the resistance in the Nazi-infested region of Norway. If he is captured, he could not only lose his life, but the lives of the fishermen and their families who join him. His mission is complicated when he falls in love with a German woman accused of betraying her Norwegian husband. In war time, love and trust are not always compatible

www.jloakleyauthor.com

Gravlaks

Yield 12-14 2 ½ oz servings

INGREDIENTS

Salt Cure
1 cup salt, kosher
¾ cup sugar
1 tbsp black pepper
1 bunch dill, fresh
Salmon
1 side of salmon fillet, deboned and skin on, about 3 lbs
juice of ½ lemon
1 oz vodka or gin, optional

DIRECTIONS

1. Mix the first three ingredients for the salt cure and set aside.
2. Place the salmon fillet in a pan large enough to lay the salmon flat.
3. Brush or rub the lemon juice over top of the fish. Then repeat with the alcohol.
4. Pack the cure evenly over top with a little less near the thinner tail. Top with the dill.
5. Add another pan the same size with some weight over top. You can use cans of beans, tomato sauce, ketchup or small 2-lb dumb bells.
6. Cure the salmon in the refrigerator for 2-3 days. The salt will start to pull out the liquid from the salmon, so every 6-8 hours drain off the liquid.
7. After 2 days, cut a small piece of the salmon and gently rinse off the cure. Slice very thin and taste. If you like it a little firmer and saltier then cure for another 12-24 hours.
8. When done, gently scrape off the salt cure. You can rinse the salmon gently under cold water as well. Then, thinly slice the salmon, holding the knife at a 30-degree angle.

Recipe Courtesy of Lisa Rovick

London, 1609. Lucy St.John, a spirited highborn orphan, is seduced by the Earl of Suffolk, and creates a powerful enemy in his beloved sister, Lady Carr. Forced to leave Court in disgrace, Lucy fights her way back into society and through an unexpected love match becomes mistress of the Tower of London, where she defies plague, intrigue, and tragic executions to tend to aristocratic prisoners and criminals alike. But with great power comes treachery, forcing Lucy to fight for her survival—and her honor—in a world of deceit and debauchery. A true story of Elizabeth St.John's ancestress from her family's surviving diaries.

www.elizabethjstjohn.com

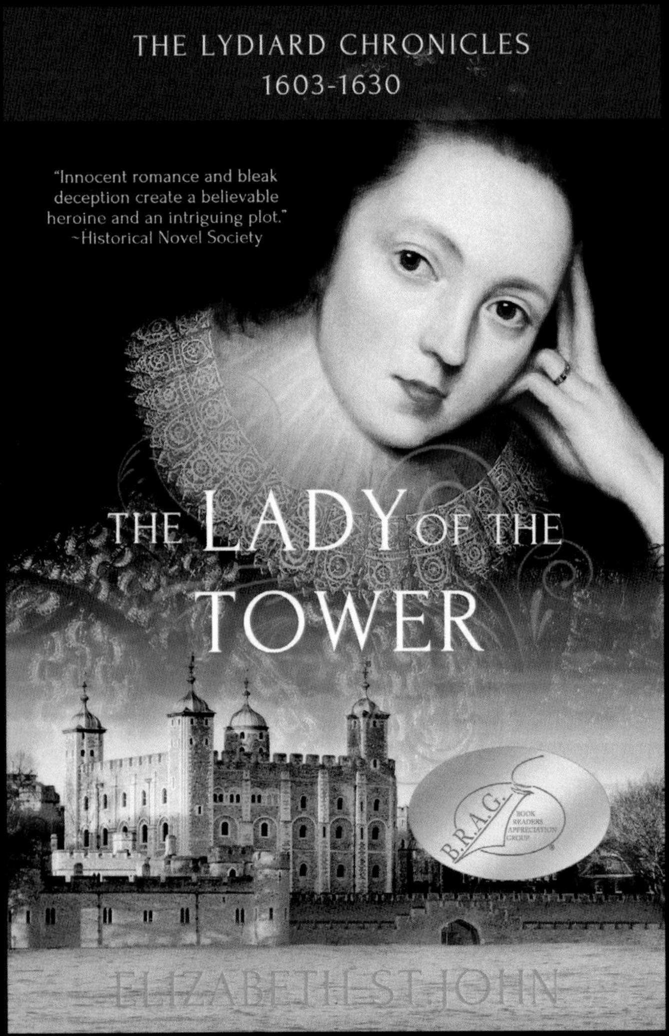

The Lady of the Tower

The "Lady" (my ancestress Lucy St. John) was an herbalist and I use recipes all the way through the book as chapter heads to set scenes. Although you may not want to share her recipe for the plagues, she was also very innovative in growing potatoes in her garden within the Tower of London.

Elizabeth St. John

Roasted Potato Lyonnaise

Serves 4

INGREDIENTS

Seasoning Spice for Potatoes
 Makes enough for 2 lbs of potatoes
 - 1 tbsp dried rosemary
 - 1 tbsp dried thyme
 - 1 tbsp garlic powder
 - 1 tbsp onion powder
 - 1 tsp black pepper, finely ground
 - 2 tsp sea salt

2 lbs potatoes, any variety, thinly sliced
3-4 tbsp potato seasoning
3 tbsp extra virgin olive oil
1 medium onion, thinly sliced

DIRECTIONS

1. Preheat oven to 400F. Line 2 large sheet trays with parchment paper.
2. Start by making the seasoning mix. Put rosemary and thyme in a coffee grinder to make into a powder. If you don't have a grinder, chop dried herbs into very small pieces.
3. Add to the rest of the spice ingredients. Stir and set aside.
4. Add potatoes, onions, seasoning mix and olive oil to a large bowl. Mix everything together, making sure the spices are well incorporated.
5. Arrange potatoes on the sheet trays in a single layer. Bake for 20 minutes then stir with a spatula. Bake another 20 minutes and stir again. Then bake for 15 minutes longer. The onions should be caramelized and the potatoes slightly golden.

This recipe is vegan and gluten free.

It is 1814, and America's second war against Great Britain is going badly. The British Crown, having driven Napoleon Bonaparte into exile, has turned its attention to the upstart United States. They seek to take New Orleans, and by doing so, control the Mississippi River and North America forever. Major Matthew Darcy is dispatched by General Andrew Jackson to help defend the beleaguered Crescent City and discovers a place that does not trust its new countrymen. Now, with a devastating invader at the city's door, Major Darcy joins a rag-tag army of backwoodsmen, Creoles, free blacks, and buccaneers in the face of overwhelming odds.

www.cajuncheesehead.com

The Plains of Chalmette

"Matthew had no idea what gumbo was. His indecision must have shown because their neighbor said in English, 'Try the gumbo, American, but stay away from the wine.'"

From *The Plains of Chalmette*

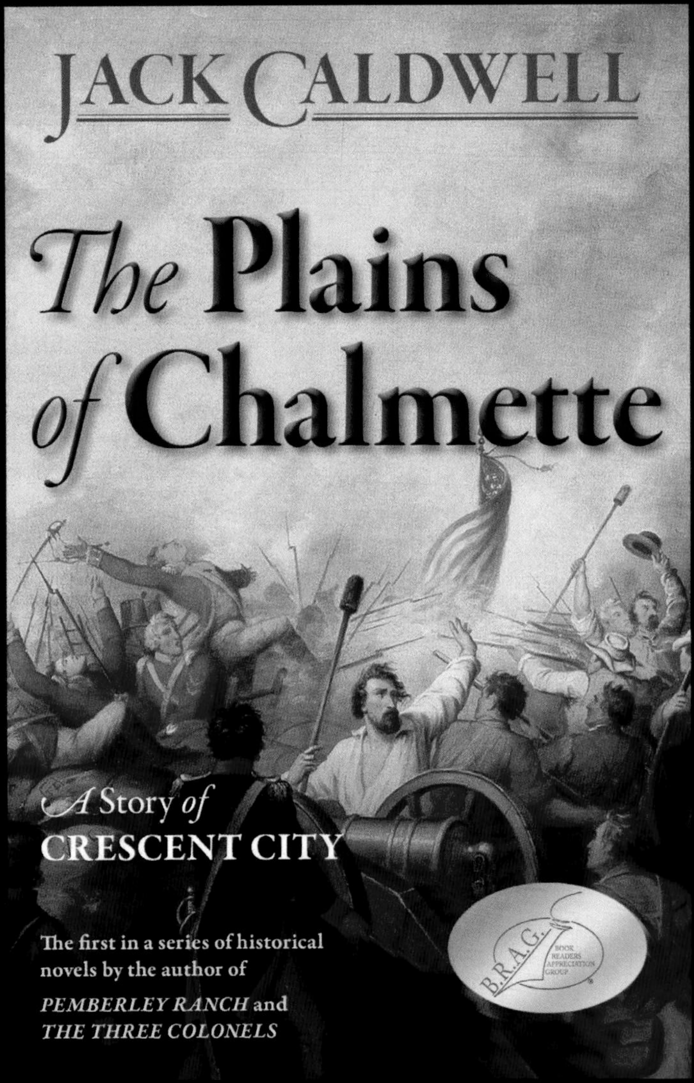

Chicken Sausage Gumbo

Serves: 4 to 6

INGREDIENTS

1 chicken, bone-in, cut into 8 pieces
salt & pepper, to taste
1 lb smoked sausage, sliced
1 cup oil
1 cup flour
1 cup onion, chopped
1 cup celery, chopped
1 cup bell pepper, chopped
4 cloves garlic, crushed
1 bay leaf
1 tbsp chili powder
1 quart chicken stock or broth
1 tsp Filé powder (optional)
½ cup parsley, minced
1 cup hot cooked white rice

DIRECTIONS

1. Season the chicken with the salt and pepper. In a stockpot brown the chicken and sausage in the oil over medium-high heat about 5-7 minutes. Remove the chicken and sausage and set aside. Lower the heat to low.
2. Make a roux by adding the flour to the pot and stirring for 20 minutes or until the mixture is the color of a penny. When the roux is the desired color, add the onion, celery, and bell pepper. Raise the heat to medium. Cook, stirring occasionally until the onions are translucent, about 10 minutes. Add garlic and cook another three minutes. Return sausage to the pot and add bay leaf and chili powder, stirring to mix.
3. Slowly pour in stock, stirring. When combined, return chicken to pot. Bring to a boil, then cover and reduce to a low heat. Simmer two hours.
4. Carefully remove the chicken and debone. Return chicken meat to pot. Heat thoroughly. Before serving, add the Filé and parsley.
5. In soup bowls, add one quarter cup of rice, then pour the gumbo over it. Serves four, with leftovers.

Recipe Courtesy of Jack Caldwell

NOTES:

- Filé powder(ground sassafras leaves) is available in gourmet grocery stores.
- Okra is not required for gumbo. If you want to use okra, put it in with the garlic and omit the Filé powder. They don't go together.
- Any smoked sausage will do. You don't need andouille. Polish kielbasa is very popular.
- You will note there is no hot sauce in the recipe. Hot sauce is for the table, not the pot.

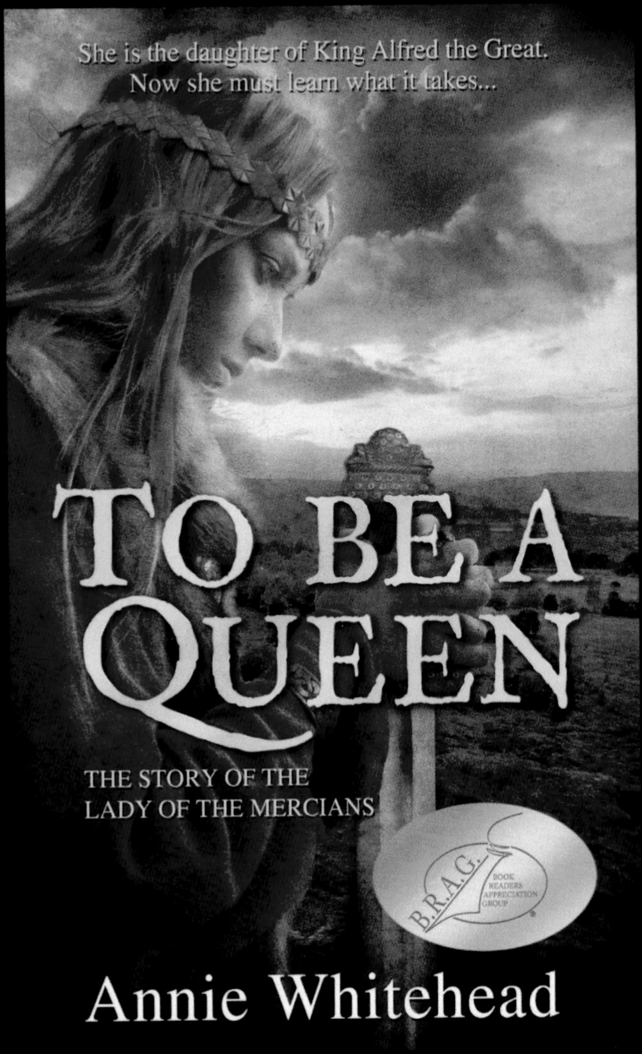

To Be A Queen

A prime rib roast is something fit for a queen! In 10th century Anglo-Saxon England, they enjoyed beef and cooked it simply on a spit over the fire. Today this would be rotisserie cooking and still is one of the tastiest of ways to cook beef.

One family, two kingdoms, one common enemy. This is the story of Æthelflæd, 'Lady of the Mercians', daughter of King Alfred the Great. Married to an older man to seal an alliance, she must earn the love of her people and overcome personal loss. When her husband falls ill, she must learn to rule and to lead an army in order to save her adopted country from the Viking onslaught and, ultimately, from her own brother. She will never have the title, but she will learn what it takes to be a queen.

www.anniewhiteheadauthor.co.uk

Rotisserie Rib Roast on grill

Serves 4-6

INGREDIENTS

4 lb prime rib roast (bones in)
Aluminum drip pan
Heavy duty gloves (for lifting the spit after cooking)
Butcher's Twine
Salt and Pepper
Olive oil

DIRECTIONS

1. The night before: Generously rub roast with olive oil and add a generous amount of salt and pepper, refrigerate
2. 2 hours before cooking: Tie twine around roast between each rib. Let sit for 2 hours to come to room temperature

Grilling

1. Heat grill to 450F – use two side burners and not the burner directly under the roast
2. Place drip pan in center beneath the roast.
3. Secure Roast onto spit skewer and place on rack- begin roasting with the lid closed.

Roasting:

1. Roasting time is approximately 1 hour- about 15 minutes per pound. Begin checking the temperature of the roast after 45 minutes
   - 115F for rare.
   - 120F in the thickest part for medium-rare
   - 125F for medium
2. Cover with foil and let stand about 15 minutes before carving.

Cook with a rotisserie attachment for your oven or barbecue or one of the many rotisserie ovens that is available to purchase.

Sauces: Serve with a sauce such as Creamy Horseradish, Mustard, Mushroom or Red Wine Sauce.

Veggies: Put vegetable in the drip pan – carrots, potatoes, onions and they will cook in the drippings.

Horror/ Paranormal Genre

Bloody Mary
Bloody Mary Cocktail

In the Hands of the Unknown
Baby Spinach and Chickpea Veggie Salad

Like To Die
Chicken Stir Fry

Tale Half Told
Wanton Cups Hors D'oeuvres

That Scoundrel Émile Dubois
Traditional English Trifle

The Muse
Dark and Stormy Night Cocktail

Bloody Mary

Mix and shake well to serve up this hilarious, upended romp about sex, love, loyalty, betrayal, and people viewed as beverages.

"What's wrong with relaxing in the evening with a little sip of wino?" asks Carakas, an alcoholic vampire whose primary concern is maintaining his buzz. But finding heavy drinkers to feast upon is a challenge. Until, that is, he meets up with Rudt, a corrupt police detective with ambitions to advance upward by eliminating his competitors. The situation is further strained by Carakas's mentor, Thedouros, who must try to keep their many enemies from killing them both...unless their friends do it first.

www.facebook.com/dackbrothers

Bloody Mary

Yield 1 Bloody Mary

INGREDIENTS

Bloody Mary Mix

¼ cup tomato or V-8 juice
1 tbsp white horseradish
1 tsp Worcestershire sauce
¼ tsp tabasco sauce
Pinch tsp celery salt
½ lime, fresh squeezed
½ lemon, fresh squeezed
1 tbsp vodka
Dash black pepper
Dash sea salt
Dash celery seeds

Cocktail

2 oz vodka
8 oz Bloody Mary mix

DIRECTIONS

1. Combine Bloody Mary mix in a pitcher. Pour 8 oz mix and vodka into a highball glass containing ice. Stir well.
2. Adjust how spicy, salty or citrusy you like it.
3. Garnish with a celery stalk, olives and cherry tomatoes on a skewer and a lemon slice.

Option:
Like it hot?
Add 5 drops hot sauce

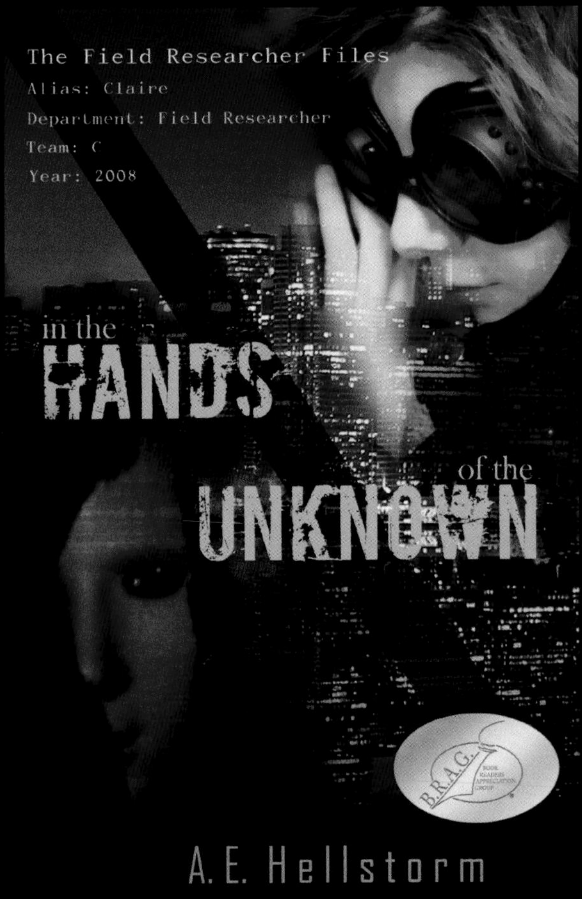

In the Hands of the Unknown

"The salad was made with lots of chickpeas, carrots, and fresh baby spinach, and an abundance of homemade dressing, and the deep red wine was poured into the glasses. Miriam was delighted. She helped her placing everything on the large table outside on the terrace so they could enjoy the last bit of sunset while eating. The air was mild and dry, and the potted flowers and herbs spread an amazing scent."

From *In the Hands of the Unknown*

FBI-agent Miriam Goldblum has seen many tragic deaths, but nothing like this. This girl had been eaten alive from the inside. For years, Miriam has worked with cases that step over the precious line of normal and throws her deep into a dark and shadowy world of supernatural crimes. Together with her team, Miriam tries to find the people responsible for the girl's death, but soon, they realize that they might become the next victims themselves. Will they be able to solve the case without horrible losses for themselves, or is this the dreaded 'last-case-scenario' they willingly are walking into?

www.hellhagproductions.com

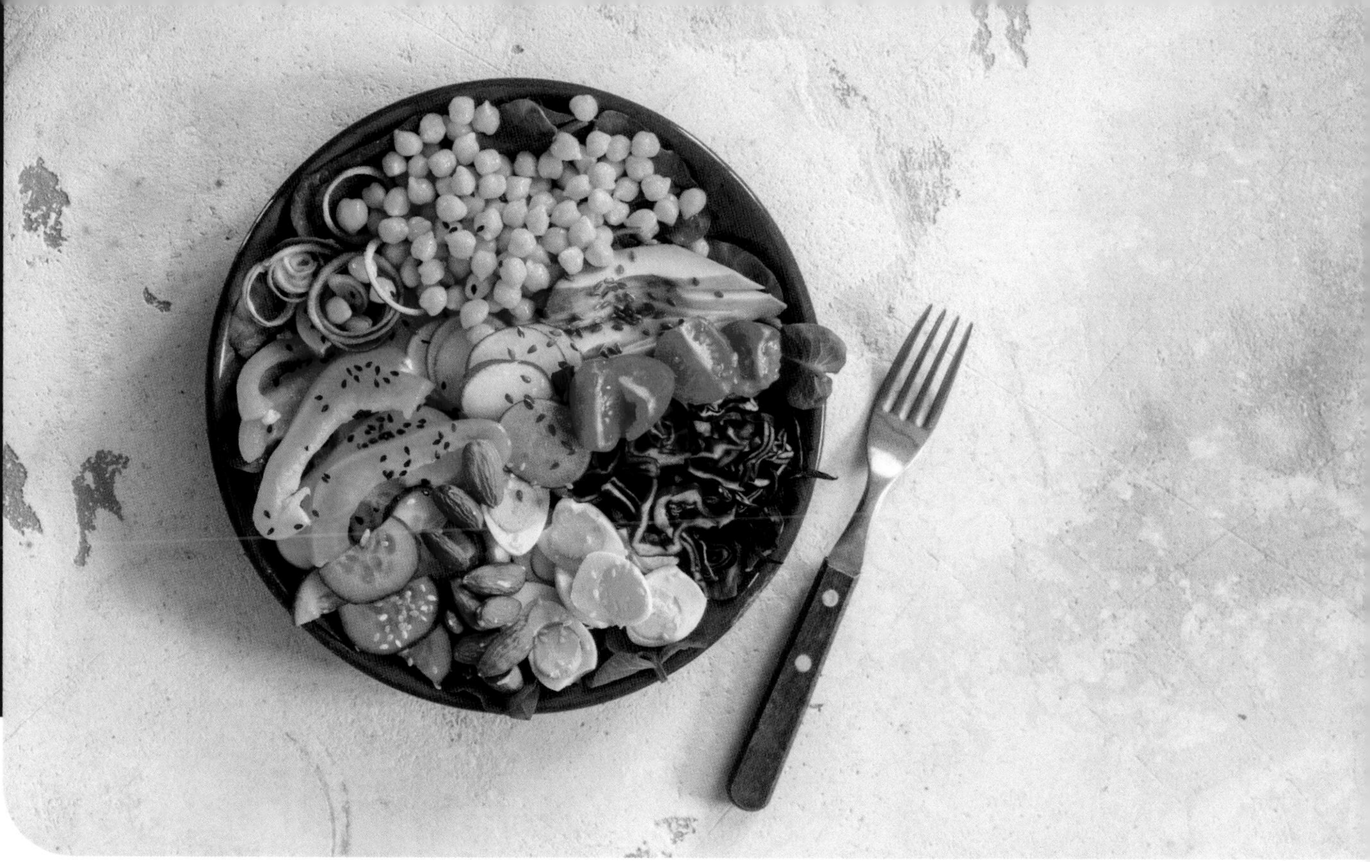

Baby Spinach and Chickpea Veggie Salad

Serves 4

INGREDIENTS

Dressing

¼ cup olive oil
¼ cup lemon Juice
1 tsp lemon zest
1 garlic clove, minced
¾ tsp salt
1 tbsp. honey
1 tsp cumin
¼ tsp pepper

Salad

1 15-oz canned chickpeas
1 sliced avocado
1 red pepper sliced
1 cucumber sliced
½ cup raw sliced almonds
2 hardboiled eggs, sliced
1 cup red cabbage, thinly sliced
½ cup red onion thinly sliced
2 cups slightly packed baby spinach

DIRECTIONS

Dressing

In a small bowl, whisk oil and lemon juice together until thickened. Add rest of ingredients and mix well. Set aside.

Salad

1. Divide spinach leaves on 4 plates.
2. Divide other ingredients and place attractively onto 4 plates.
3. Drizzle dressing on top and serve.

Like To Die

The "twenties" do not cook much. However, they do make a chicken and vegetable stir fry at home because they both want to lose some weight, and they figure stir fries are low-calorie and healthy. Vie and Carly make the stir fry and end up eating all of it, but it doesn't fill them up. They're still hungry. Carly mentions that she snuck in some cupcakes when Vie wasn't looking. They have no will power and end up devouring the cupcakes. So much for the diet!

WARNING: This isn't your typical vampire story, and Vivienne "Vie" Harper isn't your typical heroine. She's a graduate student in psychology who also works two jobs and has no time for male-patterned nonsense. When her intrusive best friend, Carly, sets her up on a date with the handsome Luke, sparks fly between them, but Luke has a secret that could threaten her life and the lives of those around her. Will Vie be able to resist him and live to survive his secret?

www.amzn.to/2HU5lW8

Beef Stir Fry to Die For

INGREDIENTS

1 lb beef or chicken, sliced into thin pieces
2 shallots, sliced thinly
1 large carrot, sliced diagonally into thin slices
2 stalks celery, sliced diagonally into thin slices
2 cups broccoli florets, cut into thin segments
8 oz snow peas
6 oz mushrooms, such as shitake or oyster
½ cup water
1½ tsp cornstarch
½ tsp granulated bouillon
2 tbsp soy sauce
1 tsp brown sugar
2 cloves garlic, minced
1 tbsp rice wine or white wine
1 tsp sesame oil
1 tsp ginger, minced
Sesame or vegetable oil, as needed
8 oz rice noodles

DIRECTIONS

1. Mise en place or Prep: Cut beef into thin pieces. If desired, marinate in 2 tablespoons of a sweet liqueur such as amaretto or Drambuie. Refrigerate until needed. Do not mix cut-up vegetables. Place them in small bowls and then stir fry each vegetable separately according to the time it needs.
2. Prepare sauce: Mix cold water and cornstarch in a measuring cup. Add granulated bouillon, soy sauce, brown sugar, garlic, wine, sesame oil and ginger. Stir and set aside.
3. Add 1 tablespoon oil to a wok or large frying pan over a high heat. Have a colander nestled in a bowl to receive the cooked vegetables. This drains excess oil from the vegetables. Place the onions in the wok and stir continuously until translucent. Remove from wok and place in colander. One at a time, add the vegetables, another tablespoon of oil if necessary, stir fry separately carrots, celery, broccoli and snow peas, removing each after they become soft or al dente (to your taste) and placing them in the colander.
4. Remove beef from refrigerator. Add 1 tablespoon oil if needed and place beef in wok, stirring continuously until beef is cooked to your desired doneness. If there is too much beef to place all at once, place a little at a time until done. Remove beef as it is done and place in a separate bowl.
5. Drain any liquid in wok. Add sauce all at once and stir continuously until it thickens. Add beef back into sauce and stir to coat. Add all other vegetables in and stir gently together. Turn off heat.
6. Cook rice noodles according to package directions. Serve on side of Beef Stir Fry or mix together.

Expandthetable suggestions:

Add other veggies of choice: bok choy, mushrooms, eggplant, bell peppers or baby corn.

Keep it vegan: Omit beef, substitute 8oz of tofu and/or add 2 cups more vegetables, such as above.

Add some heat: Add ¼ to ½ tsp cayenne pepper to the sauce mix.

Gluten Free: Substitute potato starch for cornstarch.

On December 23, 1946, Charles Reynolds murdered his pregnant wife in a houseful of party-goers, then committed suicide. Twenty-five years later, a car accident forces four friends to take shelter from an approaching storm in the abandoned Reynolds house. Newly-weds Michael and Susan Wright, and Linda and her brother, Vietnam vet, Johnny, don't believe in the supernatural - yet. The car crash wasn't an accident: they have been chosen as pawns in a dangerous battle of wills. As the darkness falls, each will be tested - fighting not only for their lives, but for their sanity.

www.killarneytraynor.com

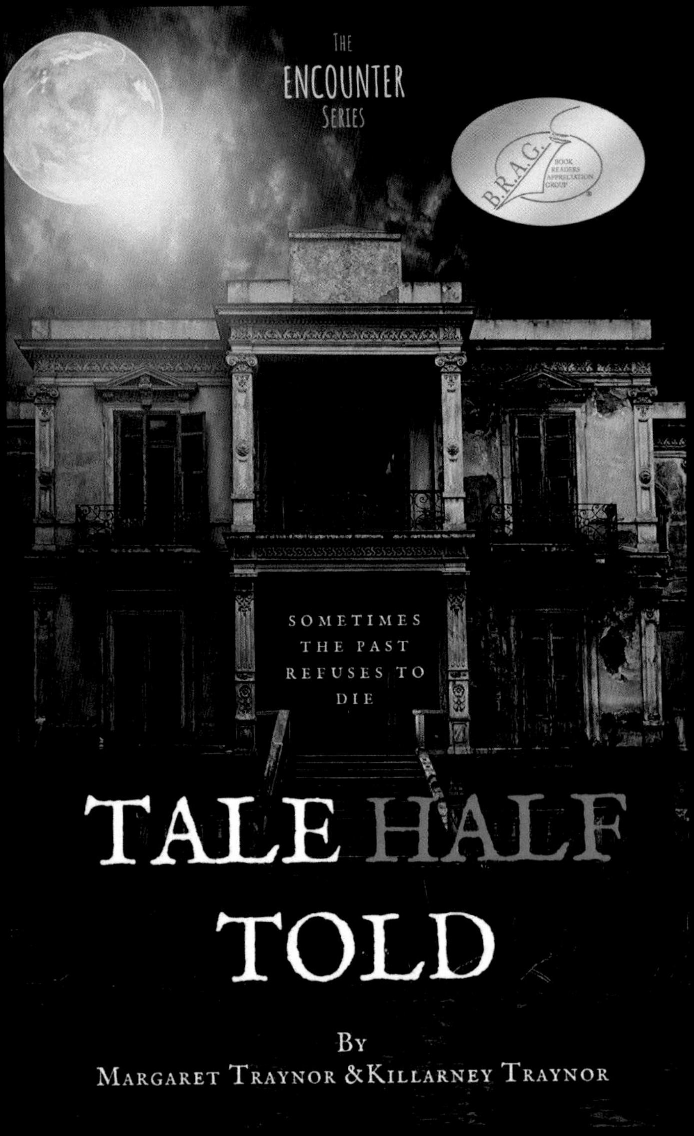

Tale Half Told

Our characters, Susan and Linda prepared finger foods for the Christmas Eve party. Along with wine and fruit cake, I'm sure these Hors D'oeuvres would be perfect.

Wonton Cups Hors D'oeuvres

24 Wanton Cups

Preheat oven to 375F. Bake wonton cups in oil sprayed muffin tins for 4-5 minutes.

SAUSAGE INGREDIENTS

1 lb sausage or chopped meat of choice
1 small onion, minced
2 garlic cloves, minced
1 bell pepper, seeded and minced
6 fresh basil leaves or ½ tsp dried basil
1 cup marinara or spaghetti sauce

DIRECTIONS

1. Sauté sausage in skillet over medium heat until browned.
2. Add onion, garlic, bell pepper and basil.
3. Add 1 cup marinara sauce.
4. Cook until mixture has thickened.
5. Add salt and pepper to taste.

Spoon 1 tbsp or so of mixture into wonton cups. Bake 5-8 minutes. Serve warm.

BROCCOLI-CHEESE. INGREDIENTS

⅔ cup broccoli chopped
⅔ cup grated cheddar or swiss cheese
⅓ cup minced chives
Salt and pepper

DIRECTIONS

1. Mix broccoli, cheese, and chives together.
2. Add salt and pepper to taste.
3. Fill wonton cups with 1 tablespoon or so mixture.
4. Bake 7-8 minutes or until broccoli is soft and cheese is melted.

The Muse

After reading this horror story you are going to need a strong drink! What could be more appropriate for a story about an author/ beast than a "Dark and Stormy night".

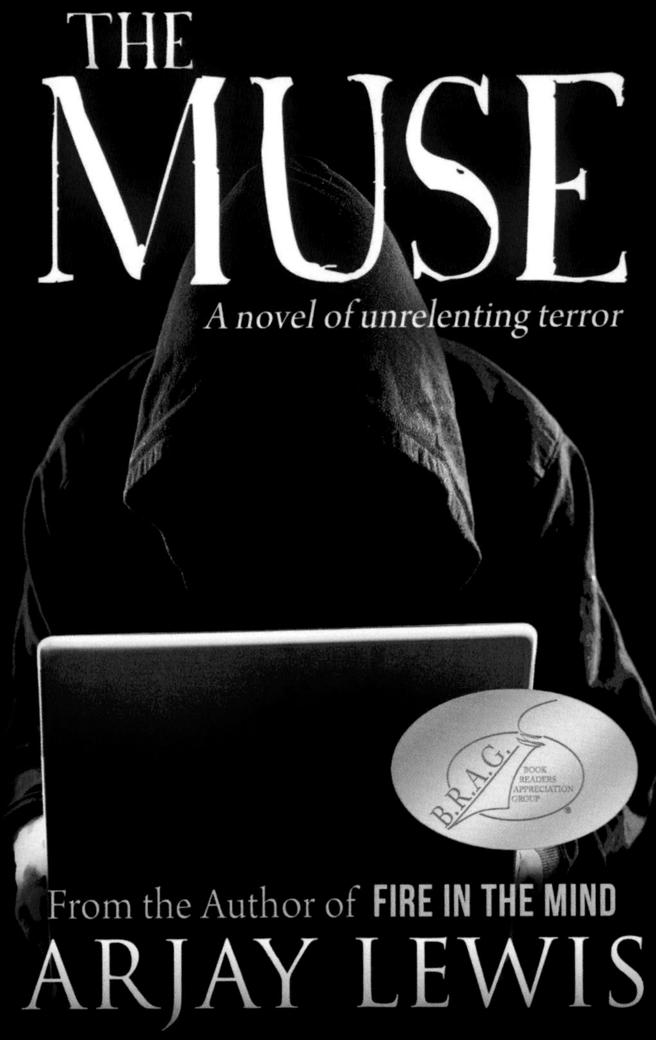

Hugely successful horror author Jack Court has a chilling secret. When he's not writing bestsellers, he murders the innocent to satisfy the twisted whims of a symbiotic creature who lives within him. But after a sheriff out for justice chases him into the path of an oncoming car, the beast escapes the writer's injured body in search of another host...

The Muse is a horror thriller that's bound to give you nightmares. If you like supernatural suspense, chilling creatures, and dark plots, then you'll love Arjay Lewis' award-winning nail-biter of a novel.

www.arjaylewis.com

Dark and Stormy Cocktail

INGREDIENTS

2 oz dark rum

3 oz ginger beer

½ oz lime juice (optional)

DIRECTION

1. Fill a glass with ice cubes.
2. Pour rum over the ice.
3. Pour in ginger beer
4. Add lime juice if desired.
5. Stir
6. Garnish with a lime wedge.

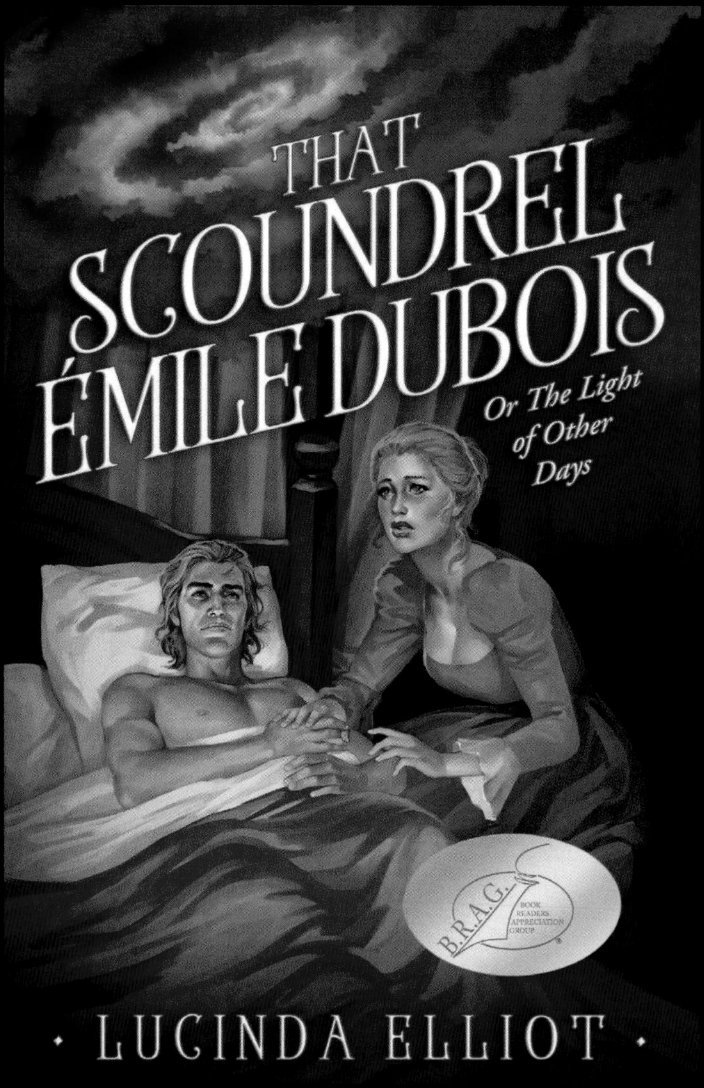

That Scoundrel Emile Dubois

Trifle first appeared in the book of English cookery in 1585 and has been a regular treat ever since. "Christmas 1794- Both Sophie and Kenrick (half Vampire) are very fond of trifle."

From *That Scoundrel Emile Dubois*

A dashing highwayman lying low from the Bow Street runners is bitten by a siren half vampire and joins with a dowager's virtuous companion in a Gothic adventure with vampires and time travel. Young Sophie de Courcy, living as a poor relative with an elderly countesses' family in an isolated mansion on the mountains in North Wales, dreams of romance and adventure, and stands little hope of finding either. When Sophie's long term hero, the rascally Émile Dubois, comes on a sudden visit to his aunt the countess, he and Sophie are drawn into a world of Gothic horror. Now Sophie has more adventure than she ever wanted.

www.sophieandemile.wordpress.com

English Christmas Trifle

The best thing about Trifle is that it is nearly fool proof! You can be creative with flavors of cakes and puddings and choose fruits and jam you love!

INGREDIENTS

2 boxes vanilla pudding mix (not instant)
pound cake or Lady fingers
strawberry jam
canned strawberries in syrup
fresh blueberries
whipping cream
fresh strawberries for garnish
¼ - ½ cup Cream Sherry

DIRECTIONS

1. Cut cake into pieces and spread with jam.
2. Layer into large bowl to fill (May take more than 1 cake).
3. Sprinkle with juice from the canned fruit and sherry.
4. Layer fruits on cake.
5. Pour pudding over to fill bowl.
6. Refrigerate.
7. Just before serving, cover top with whip cream and decorate with cherries.

Be creative:

Black Forest Trifle with chocolate cake and pudding with cherries. Springtime with mandarin oranges and orange flavoring. Christmas with crushed candy canes and peppermint flavored whip cream. Decorate with fruit, candy, chocolate shavings or sprinkles in holiday colors.

LITERARY FICTION GENRE

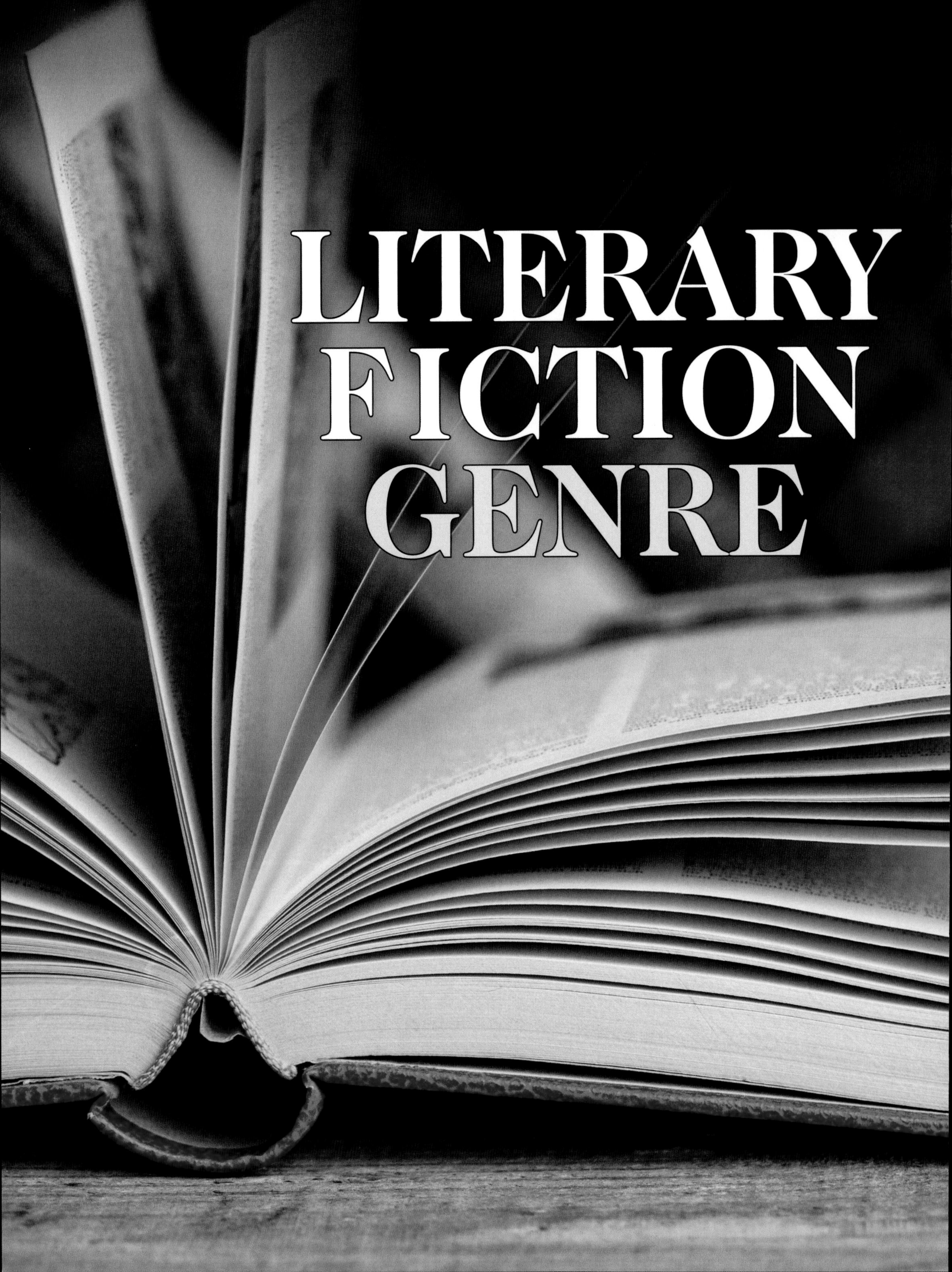

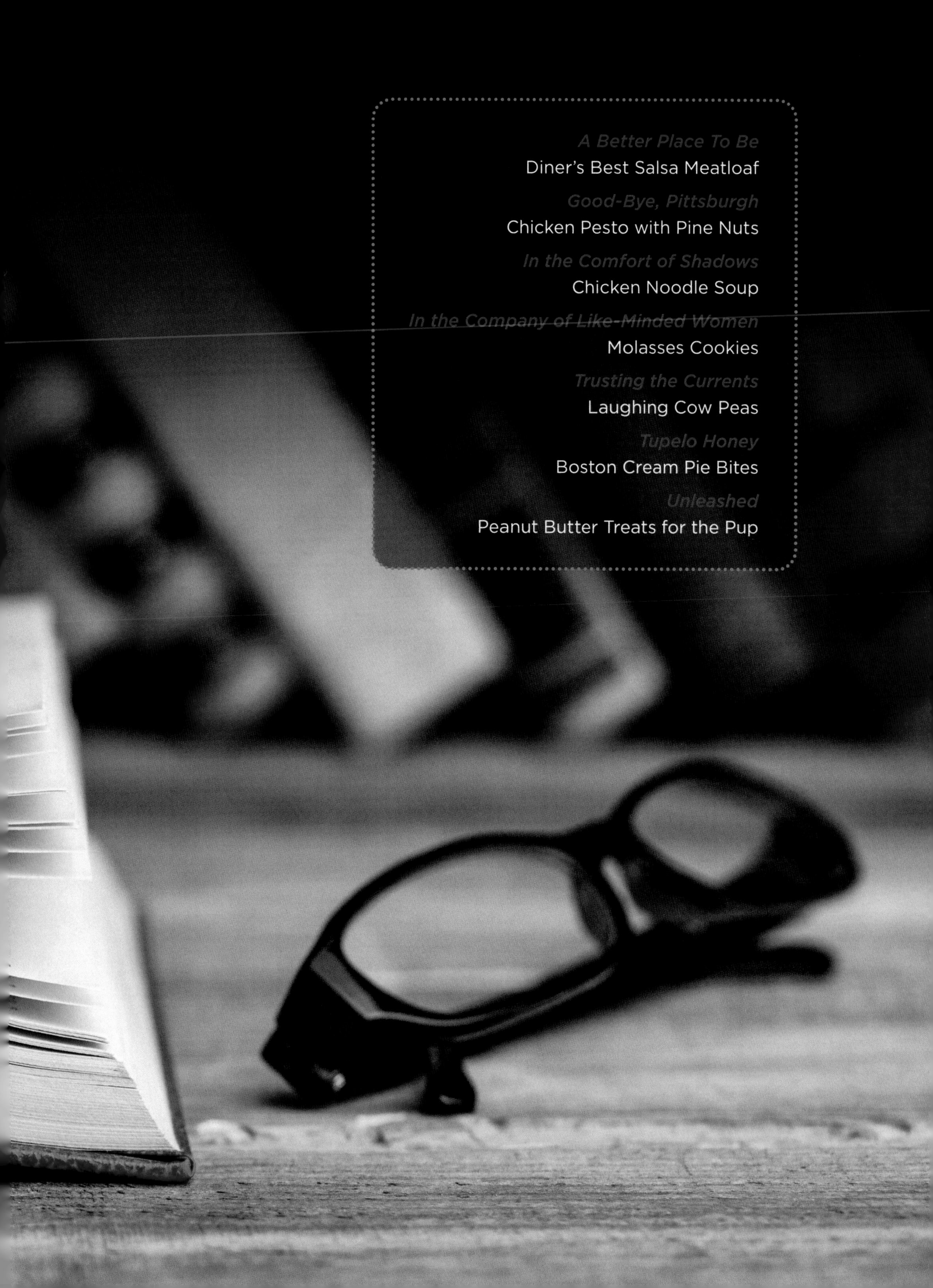

A Better Place To Be
Diner's Best Salsa Meatloaf

Good-Bye, Pittsburgh
Chicken Pesto with Pine Nuts

In the Comfort of Shadows
Chicken Noodle Soup

In the Company of Like-Minded Women
Molasses Cookies

Trusting the Currents
Laughing Cow Peas

Tupelo Honey
Boston Cream Pie Bites

Unleashed
Peanut Butter Treats for the Pup

A BETTER PLACE TO BE

Based On The Harry Chapin Song

DAVID WIND

A Better Place To Be

Because a diner plays an important part in A Better Place To Be, what better dinner could you get than Meatloaf - a down home staple?

A Novel based on the Harry Chapin song.

John and Claire have a wonderful marriage. Their love is unquestionable. Life deals John a devastating blow, as happens to far too many people, and his wife is taken from him. John's life corkscrews into an overwhelming journey to the bottom of life. There, in the darkness of his despair, a homeless drunk in trouble with the law, he wakes up in a rehab center. Forced to face both his past and possible future, John must find the path to rise from this despair and find a way to survive.

www.davidwind.com

Diner's Best Salsa Meatloaf

Serves 4-6

INGREDIENTS

1½ lbs ground turkey or beef
¾ cup of breadcrumbs
1½ tsp salt or 1 tsp Teriyaki sauce
¼ tsp pepper
1 egg, beaten
1 cup medium salsa (Any salsa will work, but the chunkier salsas with some fruit work well.)
1 tsp Worcestershire sauce
½ tsp of Montreal Steak seasoning, optional
2 tbsp ketchup or BBQ sauce of choice

DIRECTIONS

1. Heat oven to 350F.
2. In a medium bowl, using your hands or large fork, mix all ingredients together except the ketchup /BBQ sauce.
3. Use 8 ½ by 4 ½ by 2 ½ loaf pan. Drizzle bottom of pan with ketchup or BBQ sauce.
4. Fill pan with the meatloaf mixture and form into a loaf.
5. Drizzle ketchup or BBQ sauce on top.
6. Bake uncovered 1 hour or until internal temperature is at 170F.
7. Let stand 5 minutes before slicing and serving.

Expandthetable Suggestions:

Personal portions: Make meatloaf in muffin tins. Bake for 20 minutes.

In the years following America's victory over Germany and Japan, the heady exhilaration of winning the war begins to fade in post-war Pittsburgh. The spewing filth of the steel mills and the stinging aftermath of the war take their toll on the Donatti family. Better jobs await them in California, and the family plans to head west. A window into post-war America, Good-Bye, Pittsburgh is a moving tale of friendship, loyalty, and shattered dreams.

www.facebook.com/mary.l.reed.10

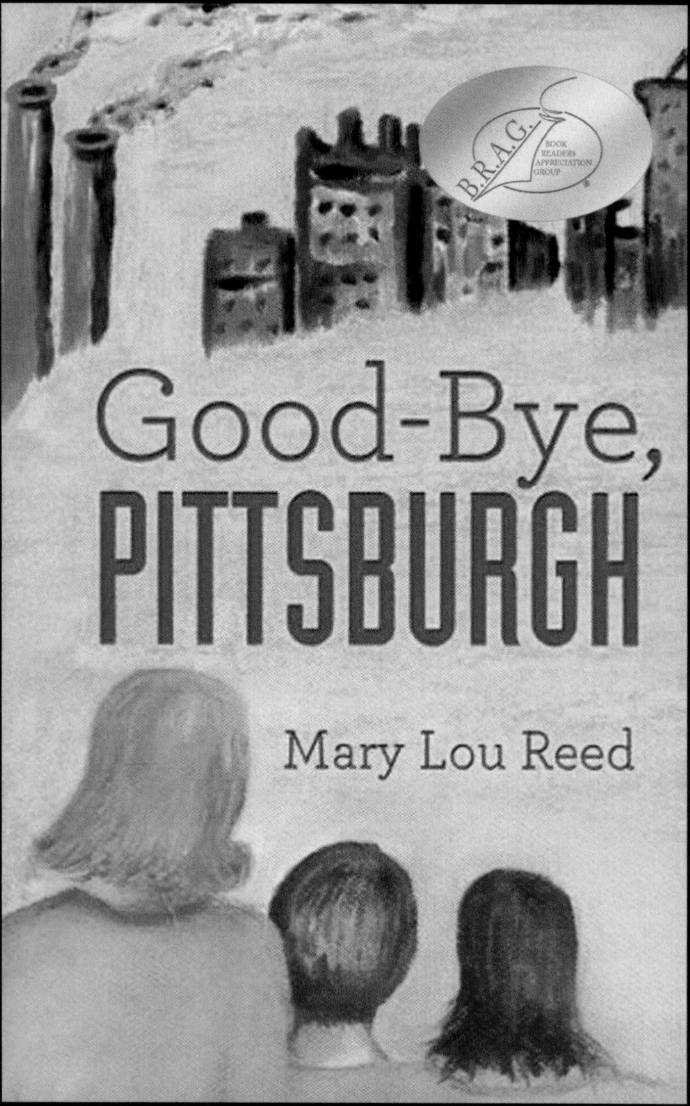

Good-Bye, Pittsburgh

The Donatti family would have carried on their Italian heritage no matter where they settled and this would include wonderful pasta dishes, sauces and cheese.

Chicken Pesto

Serves 2-3

INGREDIENTS

2 chicken breasts, boneless
1 box farfalle
¼ cup fresh basil, sliced thinly
2 cloves garlic, minced
2 tbsp pine nuts, toasted
¼ cup olive oil
1 tsp freshly squeezed lemon juice
Salt and pepper

DIRECTIONS

1. Grill chicken breasts until golden on both sides and white throughout. Remove chicken from grill. If you are grilling vegetables, you may add to the grill now. Cool chicken slightly and slice into thin strips.
2. Boil farfalle according to package instructions. Drain.
3. Toss pasta with basil, garlic, and olive oil. Squeeze lemon juice on top. Mix. Add chicken and toss gently. Taste and adjust seasoning.

Photo Courtesy of Susan Weintrob

In the Comfort of Shadows

In the Comfort of Shadows takes place during winter in rural northern Wisconsin. Is there anything more comforting on a cold winter's day than Chicken Noodle Soup? Pair it with a grilled cheese sandwich (Wisconsin Cheese of course!) and you have the perfect meal.

In the Comfort of Shadows tells of how Ann Olson's search for the identity of her birth parents leads her to Emmett Pederson, an elderly, reclusive farmer in rural Wisconsin who may be her "father unknown." Ann knows Emmett is her adoptive dad's cousin and that the family abandoned Emmett years ago. But since memories of childhood days on Emmett's farm haunt her, Ann sets out to face him, unaware she'll find herself, her sister, and their mother named in Emmett's WW2 diary and unprepared for falling in love with a local man who helps her find strength in forgiveness.

https://amzn.to/3cwm9Aq

Comforting Chicken Noodle Soup

Serves 4 as a meal or more for a start

INGREDIENTS

1-2 tbsp olive oil
1 large onion, diced
2 garlic cloves, minced
2-4 stalks celery, chopped
1 medium zucchini, chopped (peel if desired)
2 large carrots, chopped (peel if desired)
1-2 lbs uncooked chicken, any part
1 tbsp Kosher salt
Pepper to taste
Water to cover chicken and vegetables
½ lb noodles of choice
* Frugal people like Emmett would use up what's in the refrigerator: Add other vegetables on hand, such as parsnips, turnips, potatoes or corn.

DIRECTIONS

1. Wash vegetables and peel zucchini and carrots, if desired.
2. Sauté onion, garlic, celery and zucchini until softened.
3. Put sautéed vegetables and rest of ingredients, except the noodles, in a large pot and bring to a boil. Reduce heat and partially cover, simmering for 2 hours. Add more liquid if required.
4. Some people remove vegetables from soup or leave them in. Your choice.
5. Take chicken out of pot and remove meat. Shred. Return shredded chicken meat to soup.
6. Cook noodles according to package directions, drain and add to soup. Adjust seasoning.
7. Serve with a homemade or good store-bought crusty bread.

In the Company of Like-Minded Women explores the complexities of bonds between sisters and family at the start of the 20th century when women struggled to determine their future and the "New Woman" demanded an equal voice. Three sisters are reunited in 1901 Denver following a family rift many years before. Each sister faces critical decisions regarding love, work, and the strength of her convictions. The success of Colorado women in gaining the right to vote in 1893–twenty-seven years before the passage of national suffrage–and their continued fight for women's rights, provides the background as the story unfolds.

www.elainerussell.info

In the Company of Like-Minded Women

"Two of my favorite people were Angela, our cook, and her daughter, Chastity, two years older than me, who helped her mother in the kitchen. Chastity and I often played house together in the warm, smoky spaces near the brick oven, sharing my porcelain doll and her rag doll. We held tea parties with glasses of fresh lemonade and her mother's molasses cookies."

From *In the Company of Like-Minded Women*

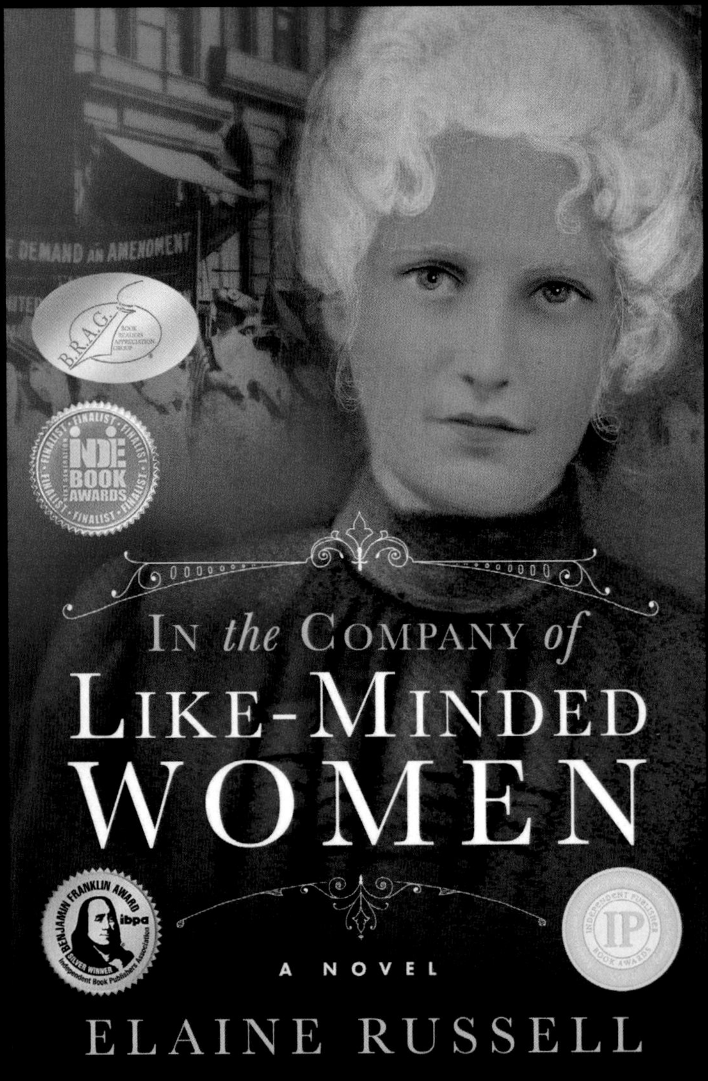

Molasses Sugar and Spice Cookies

INGREDIENTS

¾ cup butter
1 cup sugar
1 egg
¼ cup molasses
2 cups flour
2 tsp baking soda
¼ tsp salt
1 tsp cinnamon
¼ tsp ground cloves
¾ tsp dry ginger

DIRECTIONS

1. Line baking sheet with parchment paper. Preheat oven to 375F.
2. Cream butter and sugar together. Add egg and molasses and stir.
3. Mix dry ingredients together in separate bowl, then add to liquid mixture and stir to make soft dough.
4. Drop in large teaspoon rounds onto cookie sheet.
5. Bake for 10 to 12 minutes at 375F. When cooled, but still a tiny bit warm, dip the top of cookies in powdered sugar.

Recipe Courtesy of Elaine Russell

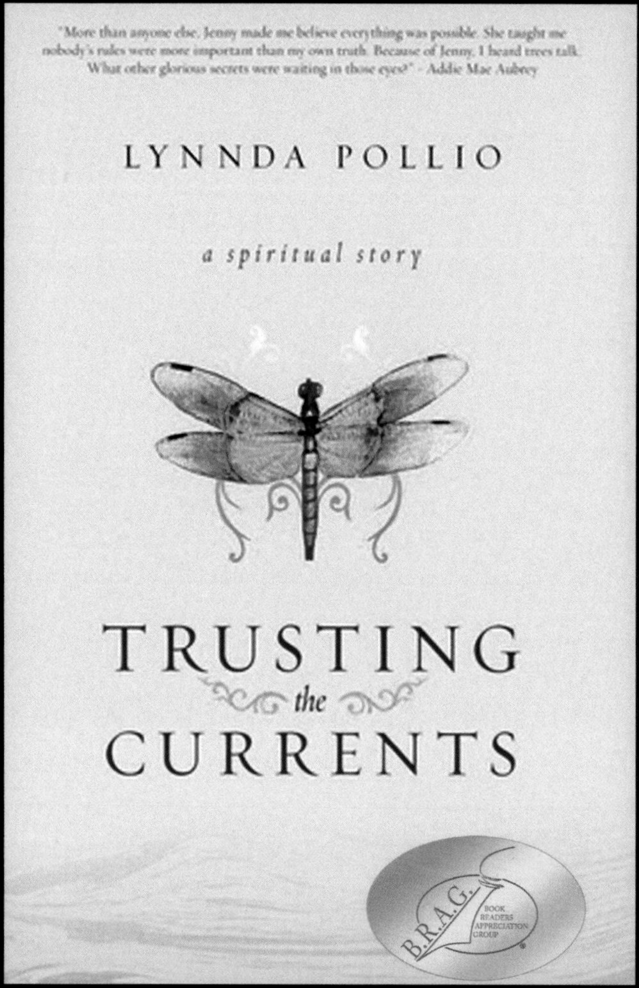
"More than anyone else, Jenny made me believe everything was possible. She taught me nobody's rules were more important than my own truth. Because of Jenny, I heard trees talk. What other glorious secrets were waiting in those eyes?" - Addie Mae Aubrey
LYNNDA POLLIO
a spiritual story
TRUSTING the CURRENTS
B.R.A.G.
BOOK READERS APPRECIATION GROUP

Trusting the Currents

Mama's go-to-dinner recip is her secret Laughing Cow Peas, a dinner that Addie Mae ruins. Jenny's a better cook, as Addie Mae says, "Best thing about Jenny's cooking was that it healed much as satisfied."

From *Trusting the Currents*

Narrated by Addie Mae Aubrey, Trusting the Currents is a story of self-discovery, of faith, courage, and the uneasy search for one's place in life. Beginning at age eleven with the arrival of beautiful, mysterious cousin Jenny and her shadowy stepfather, Uncle Joe, Trusting the Currents explores Addie Mae's reluctant awakening. As Jenny introduces Addie Mae to the natural world, a caring teacher guides Addie Mae with the power of reading. Romantic love enters her life for the first time with Rawley, and we experience how Addie Mae's emerging sense of self compels her to a life-altering decision, even as evil shakes all of their lives.

Mama's Laughing Cow Peas

Serves 6-8

INGREDIENTS

1 package favorite noodles or pasta
1 tbsp olive oil, butter, margarine
3 cups frozen peas or fresh
1 ½ cups shredded cheese
⅓ cup cream or milk
3 sprigs fresh parsley or ½ tsp dried

DIRECTIONS

1. Make noodles according to recipe. Before you drain the noodles, stir in the peas, then drain.
2. Put noodles and peas in a large bowl. Add parsley. Season with salt and pepper according to taste.
3. Over low heat, add milk or cream to a pot and add in cheese, stirring until thickened.
4. Pour over noodles and toss gently. Correct seasoning.

Recipe Courtesy of Lynnda Pollio

Tupelo Honey

Tupelo LOVES food. She loves pies, sweets and candies. Boston Crème Pie to be specific!

Could she resist these creamy bites of cake smothered in chocolate?

Set in rural Mississippi, with a cast of colorful southerners, it stars one pretty dysfunctional family at the center of which is Tupelo Honey. To paraphrase Tolstoy, it's the unhappy families that are unique -- and by definition, often more interesting. Tupelo Honey does not have an easy life, on the surface. Her mother is a drug addict, and mental illness lingers in her grandmother Marmalade's house like a hot humid August cloud. It's certainly not a dull life, one full of heartbreaks big and small, but this tough sweet girl pulls it off with aplomb. It's a treat from start to end.

www.lisannalangston.com

Boston Cream Pie Bites

CAKE INGREDIENTS

1 box of Yellow cake mix
Use non-dairy milk instead of dairy milk.

To save time, you can make the yellow cake ahead of time and refrigerate or freeze

DIRECTIONS

1. Bake in muffin tins or in a thin layer in baking sheets. Cool.
2. Cut muffins in half. If using the sheets, cut into 2" or 3" squares.
3. Place bottoms on a dish or pan. Take a tablespoon of the refrigerated custard and spoon over cake. Gently place top over the custard.

NON-DAIRY CUSTARD INGREDIENTS

Yield 5 cups

3 cups unsweetened almond milk
1 cup cream of coconut
1 stick cinnamon
Finely grated rind from 1 lemon
4 egg yolks
¾ cups sugar
3 tbsp cornstarch
1 tsp vanilla extract

DIRECTIONS

1. Heat over medium heat, warm almond milk and cream of coconut, cinnamon stick and lemon rink together in a pot until bubbles start to form on the sides.
2. In a medium size bowl, beat egg yolks and sugar until pale yellow. Add corn starch and keep beating until entirely smooth.
3. Add vanilla extract and beat until smooth and creamy. Remove cinnamon stick. Slowly add about ½ cup of warm milk to the egg yolks, stirring constantly.
4. Add rest of milk and stir until well incorporated.
5. Return mixture to stove and cook at low to medium heat until it thickens slightly and coats the back of a wood spoon. Do not bring to boil.
6. Cool and refrigerate in a bowl if for filling. Or pour into small dishes for individual portions.

Chocolate Glaze

Yield: ½ cup

6 squares semi-sweet chocolate

½ cup water

1. Melt chocolate in water over medium heat, stirring constantly to blend.
2. Cool a bit but not until the chocolate solidifies. Spread or drizzle over top layer of the yellow cake.
3. For added custardy flavor, drizzle custard over top and sides. Refrigerate before serving.

Make it dairy: Use 4 cups of whole milk.

Expandthetable Suggestions:

Make it sugar free: Glaze: use sugar free chocolate. Yellow cake: use stevia in place of sugar. Custard: Use 1/4 cup plus 1 tablespoon Stevia in place of sugar. To further reduce sugar, use almond milk totally and eliminate the cream of coconut.

Keep it gluten free: Custard: Substitute potato starch for cornstarch. Yellow cake: Use a gluten free flour to make cake.

Make it muffin tins: For a nice round shape and easy assembly, make yellow cake recipe in muffin tins.

Make it dairy: Use 4 cups milk or cream instead of almond and coconut milk.

Unleashed

A pup like Zephyr deserves a treat and nothing could be more full of love than a homemade dog cookie!

Eleven-year-old Rowan Graham wrestles with depression. Carolina, her mother, suggests a dog. Rowan chooses a wolfhound-deerhound mix and believes she and the pup, Zephyr, communicate. Her mom discourages this preposterous idea. During a multi-car accident, Zephyr bolts into the Central Oregon wilds. Medics airlift comatose Rowan to Portland. Nightmares haunt author Moss Westbury, Afghanistan veteran. He writes to expunge demons. When howling rekindles nightmares, he searches for the culprit on his isolated land. Unleashed is a story of courage and love, told through the eyes of Moss, Rowan, Carolina, and Zephyr—each struggling to resolve challenges and fears.

www.skyeblaine.com

Homemade Dog Treats

INGREDIENTS

1 cup pumpkin puree or sweet potato
½ cup peanut butter
2 eggs
2 cups whole wheat flour (some dogs can actually be allergic to gluten found in white flour)
½ tsp cinnamon
optional Honey
Cookie cutters can be purchased in the shape of dog bones or use fun shapes for holidays.

DIRECTIONS

1. Preheat oven to 350F. Prepare baking sheet with parchment paper.
2. In a bowl, combine pumpkin, eggs, and peanut butter.
3. Add in flour and cinnamon – mix until well combined.
4. Roll out dough on floured surface.
5. Cut shapes out of dough with cookie cutters and place on prepared baking sheet.
6. Bake for 20 minutes. Cook longer to get a crunchier biscuit

These treats can be frozen.

MIDDLE GRADE GENRE

Andee the Aquanaut
Tropical Fruit Smoothie

Daisy, Bold & Beautiful
Maple Braised Brussels Sprouts with Red Onions

Left Out
Welsh Rarebit

Little Miss History Travels to Mount Vernon
Colonial Southern Stew

Misha Alexandrov
Russian Blini with Smoked Salmon

My Magical Kippah
Chanukah Root Vegetable Latkes

The Pretender
Baked Coulommiers

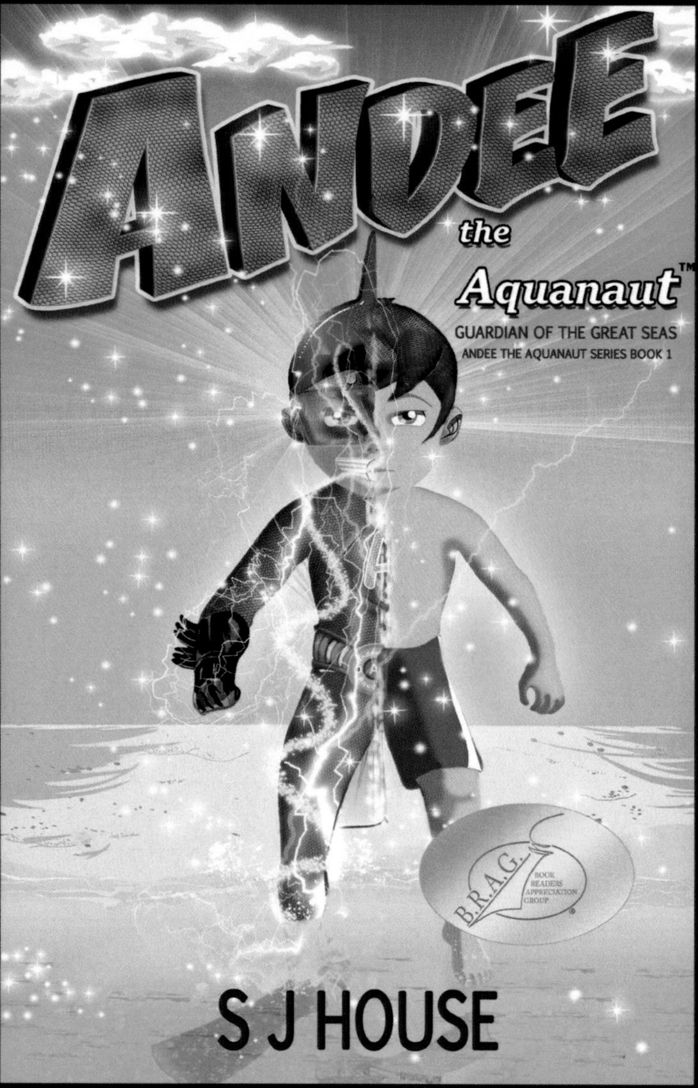

Andee the Aquanaut

Life on an Island would not be complete without a wonderful tropical drink! With the abundance of amazing fruit, these smoothies would be irresistible.

Exploring the underwater world of the lost city. Andee meets the Wise White Dolphin. Andee has been given special powers, allowing him to become one of the great and legendary Aquanauts of the Marine Kingdom. Many quests and adventures await him - his purpose at first is to assist and protect all marine life.

www.simonjhouse.com

Tropical Fruit Smoothie

INGREDIENTS

1 cup coconut milk
1 cup mangoes, fresh or frozen
1 banana
½ cup pineapple cubed
½ cup halved strawberries
Handful of fresh spinach
1 slice kiwi with a sprig of mint for garnish.

DIRECTIONS

1. Starting with the liquids, put all the ingredients in the blender, except for the garnish.
2. Purée until smooth.
3. Add kiwi with a sprig of mint for garnish

This is a vegan recipe.

D.J. and her dad moved far from the small town and only home she ever knew. Now she's starting middle school in the city with kids she's never met. She tries to make friends, but they all appear to be slaves to screen time. D.J. just likes to garden, nurturing plants, watching them grow and thrive. It seems she'll never find a way to fit in, but then she awakens in a gorgeous garden and meets Persephone, Goddess of Spring. Could a Greek goddess possibly help with middle school gamers?

www.authorelliecollins.wixsite.com/mysite

Daisy Bold & Beautiful

Persephone is the Greek goddess of spring and summer, so it makes perfect sense to feature a recipe for vegetables. Ellie Collins, the author, is a big fan of Brussel Sprouts!

Maple Braised Brussels Sprouts with Red Onions

Serves 6 as a side.

INGREDIENTS

1 lb Brussels Sprouts, quartered
2 tbsp olive oil
½ red onion, small dice
¼ cup maple syrup
Salt and pepper

DIRECTIONS

1. Preheat oven to 400F. Line a sheet tray with parchment paper.
2. Heat a pan on medium high heat and add olive oil. Add the onion. Sauté for a few minutes until onions soften.
3. Add Brussels Sprouts, maple syrup, salt and pepper. Stir until combined.
4. Remove from heat and transfer to sheet tray. Roast for 20 minutes or until golden and crisp.

Left Out

Being left-handed hasn't always been easy when you need to use right-handed equipment. Cooking is a perfect example. However, have no fear there is now no limit to the many cooking utensils and equipment made specifically for left-handed people!

Author Jean Gill is Welsh so how about a traditional Welsh dish that is easy enough for a teen to make- perhaps without the lager!

Award-winning modern classic of friendship and teen life, with all its pitfalls and challenges and a must for all left-handers. Being different isn't easy but it can be exciting! How well do you know your friends? Are they left-handed or right-handed? Left-brained or right-brained? And what difference does it make? Shocked at discovering how left-handers are persecuted, Jamie ties her hand behind her back for a public protest in school. This does not go down well.

www.jeangill.com

Welsh Rarebit

Serves 6

Expandthetable Suggestions:

To make alcohol free: Use apple juice in place of beer.

INGREDIENTS

2 tbsp butter
2 tbsp flour
⅓ cup milk
½ cup beer
½ tsp dry mustard
½ tsp salt
½ tsp black pepper
2 dashes Worcestershire sauce
2 cups sharp Cheddar Cheese, grated
2 egg yolks
6-8 slices of good thick bread
Chives or leeks chopped for garnish if desired

DIRECTIONS

1. Melt butter in saucepan over low heat.
2. Add flour and whisk together until combined. Cook for 2 minutes.
3. Pour in milk and beer, whisking constantly. Cook for another minute.
4. Add mustard, salt, and pepper. Whisk together. Add cheese and whisk, cooking for 2- 3 minutes until smooth and melted.
5. Remove from heat and add egg yolks. Pour cheese mixture over toast. Place in broiler for 2-3 minutes. Cut bread in half and serve immediately.

Who was George Washington? Washington is best known as America's first president, but he was also a military hero. If you asked George Washington what he really wanted to be, he would reply, "a farmer." Seeking to revolutionize antiquated 18th-century farming methods, Washington experimented with crop rotation, fertilizers, plowing, and plants. The Mount Vernon Ladies Association began restoring his estate to its former glory in 1853. Today the buildings, grounds and The Donald W. Reynolds Museum and Education Center reveal the real Father of the United States of America.

www.bamauthor.me

Little Miss History Travels to Mount Vernon

Stews were common in Colonial times. In fact, stew pans were found in the collection at Mount Vernon, showing that this meal was served by the Washingtons for family and their guests. Vegetables from the extensive gardens would have been used. In these stews they would have also used pork, chicken, venison and additional vegetables in season.

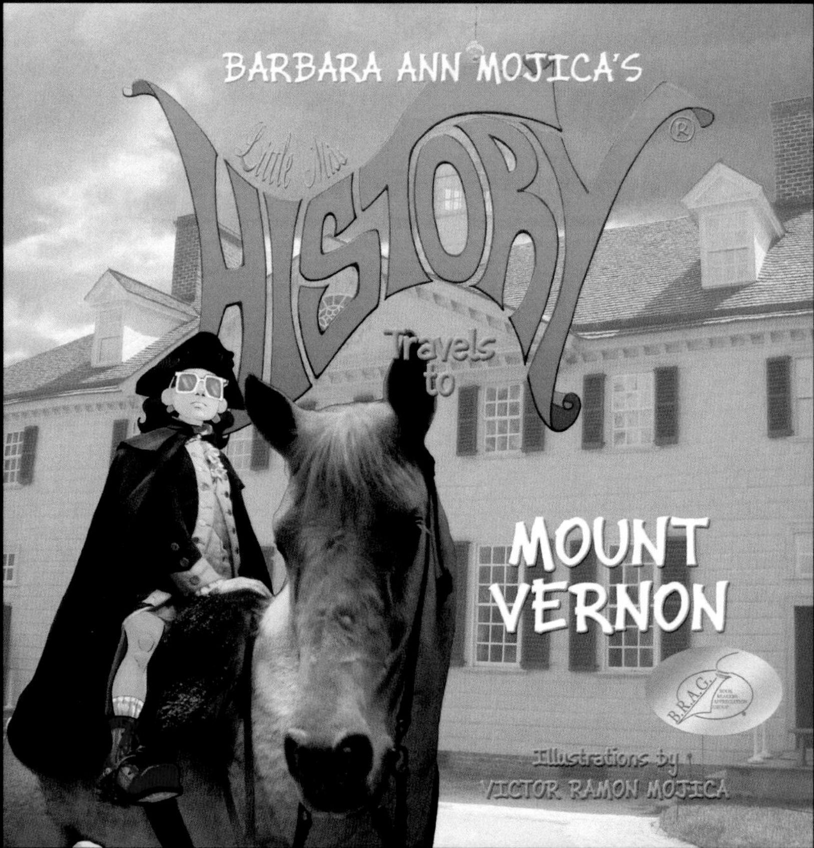

Colonial Southern Stew

Serves 6

INGREDIENTS

2 lbs stewing beef, cubed beef
3 tbsp flour
2 tsp salt
½ tsp ground pepper
3 tbsp olive oil or butter
1 onion, sliced thinly
2 garlic cloves, minced
3 stalks celery, sliced
3 carrots, sliced
8 oz mushrooms of choice, sliced
1 16-oz canned whole tomatoes
¼ cup dry red wine
1 tbsp sugar
2 sprigs fresh thyme or ¼ tsp dried
Parsley for garnish, optional

DIRECTIONS

1. Dredge beef in flour, salt and pepper. Shake off extra flour. Warm olive oil in large skillet. Add beef and brown. Remove and set aside.
2. Add onions and cook until transparent. Add garlic, celery and carrots and cook until garlic browns slightly. Remove from pan and place in casserole pan or crock pot.
3. Add more olive oil if needed. Sauté mushrooms until browned and liquid is reduced. Add to vegetables. Mash tomatoes and add to vegetables. Season with sugar, salt, pepper and thyme and gently mix.
4. Place 3 bacon slices and beef on top of vegetables and add wine. Cover and place in 350F oven and cook for 2-3 hours or until tender. If using crockpot, cook on low for 6-7 hours. Check both a few times to make sure there is enough liquid. Add a bit of water or broth if dry.
5. Serve over rice and with a few slices of cornbread on the side.

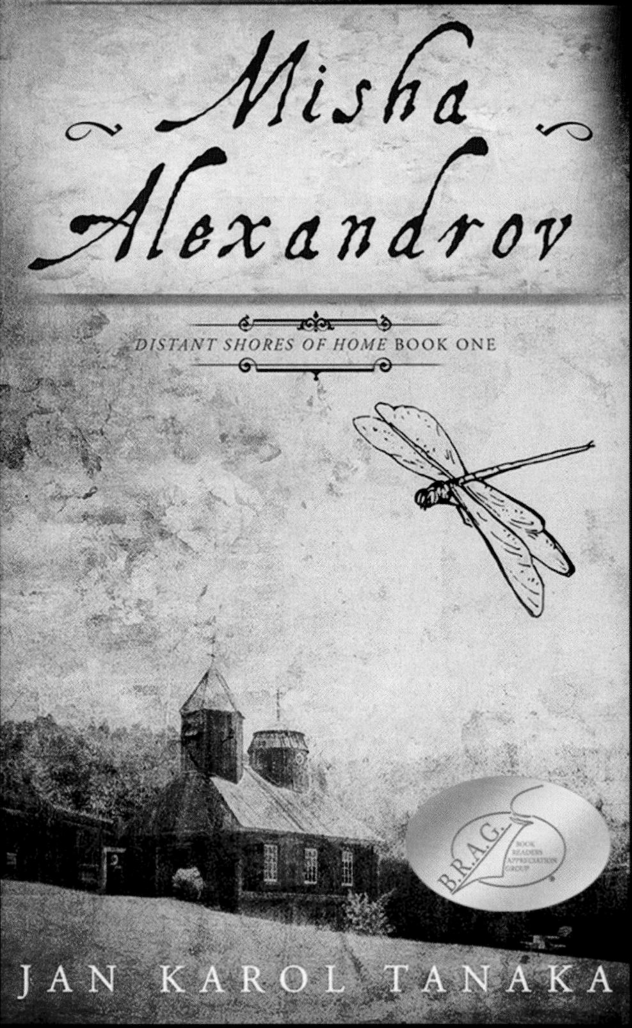

Misha Alexandrov

One of the foods that Misha Alexandrov would have probably found as a member of the Russian community in California are blinis with smoked salmon. A favorite everywhere you find Russian influence in dining.

In the spring of 1827, Misha Alexandrov arrives at Fort Ross as a ten-year-old orphan of a Russian father and an Aleut mother. Hated by the foreman for his half-breed heritage, he must prove his worth as a working member of the Russian American Company and overcome the perception that he brings with him "a bag of bad luck". On the remote coast of Alta California, a passion for the land takes root in his young heart, and he vows to do anything it takes to make the fortress colony his home.

www.samanthastclaire.com/misha-alexandrov

Russian Blini with Smoked Salmon

Expandthetable Suggestions:

Try smoked salmon with a dill mustard or use a non-dairy sour cream with chives.

Yield 8-10 blini

INGREDIENTS

2 cups all-purpose flour
1 tsp salt
1 tsp sugar
½ tsp baking powder
2 large eggs
2 ½ cups milk of choice
2 tbsp melted butter
Toppings
Cream Cheese and Smoked Salmon (Lox)
Try also Sour Cream and Chives

DIRECTIONS

1. Mix together flour, salt, sugar and baking powder.
2. Beat eggs, milk and melted butter.Add to flour mixture.
3. Mixture should be on the thin side. Refrigerate for 1 hour. Stir and check consistency. Add milk if too thick.
4. Heat butter in a skillet over a medium heat. Pour about ¼ cup of the batter into the skillet, rotating it until the batter covers the bottom of the pan. Cook until the batter begins to bubble. Cook until underside is golden and flip. Cook for 30 seconds more. Brush pan with butter. Repeat with the rest of the batter.
5. Fold blini into quarters. Top with Smoked Salmon slices and a bit of cream cheese if desired. You might also like sour cream and chives as a topping.

My Magical Kippah is about a young boy named Avram who is preparing for his upcoming Bar Mitzvah. With his voice starting to change, Avram is even more nervous about standing in front of his family and the entire congregation of his Temple to chant prayers. Avram's Zadi gifts him with a "magical" kippah that not only changes his life, but also the lives of those around him. This book is a heartwarming story for the entire family to enjoy.

www.kandimsiegel.com

My Magical Kippah

Latkes are a traditional tasty treat and are sometimes called levivot in Hebrew. Latkes are one of the most famous Jewish foods going back to at least the Middle Ages and are a specialty of Chanukah.

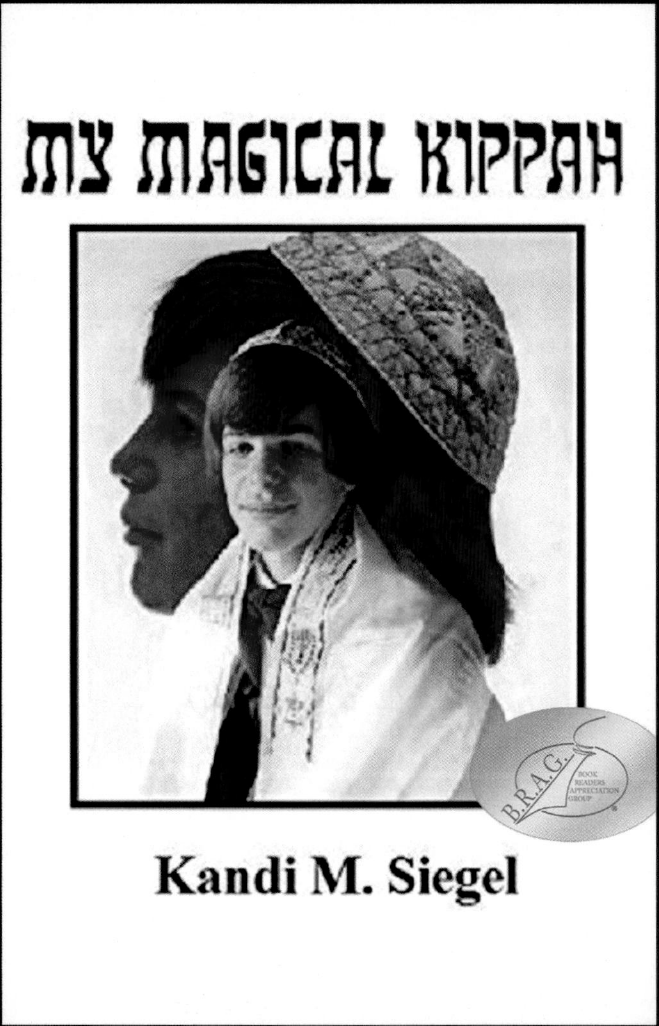

Chanukah Root Vegetable Latkes

INGREDIENTS

1 lb Yukon gold potatoes
1 lb sweet potatoes
2 carrots
2 parsnips
1 tsp. kosher salt
½ tsp. black pepper

DIRECTIONS

1. Line two baking sheets with paper towels and set aside.
2. Peel potatoes, sweet potatoes, carrots, and parsnips and coarsely grate them. Put the grated vegetables in a colander, squeeze out as much liquid as possible. Discard the liquid.
3. Place the vegetables in a mixing bowl. Stir in the next seven ingredients. Mix well. The mixture should be loose but still hold together. Add a little more flour if necessary.
4. Heat a large nonstick skillet over medium-high heat. Add enough oil to just cover the bottom of the pan, about ⅛ inch deep. When the oil is hot and shimmering, drop 2-3 tablespoon of the mixture in the skillet (per latke). Gently flatten them with a spatula to make a "pancake" three inches in diameter. Cook for three or four minutes per side, or until golden.
5. Transfer the latkes to the paper towel-lined baking sheets and sprinkle with a little salt. Repeat with the rest of the mixture, adding more oil as needed. Preheat the oven to 350F.
6. Remove the paper towels from the baking sheets, place the latkes on the baking sheets, and reheat them in the oven for five to seven minutes, or until hot. Keep the latkes in a single layer so that they crisp back up in the oven.
7. Serve with sour cream and chives, applesauce or Pecan-Date chutney.

Pecan-Date Chutney

(Yields 2 cups)

INGREDIENTS

½ cup chopped pecans
12 pitted dates, such as Medjool
1 tbsp cranberry juice
1 tbsp red currant jelly or raspberry jam
Pinch of kosher salt

DIRECTIONS

Place all ingredients in a food processor. Pulse until just combined. The mixture should have texture. Place in a bowl and set aside.

Tip: The chutney can be made a day or two ahead of time, covered, and refrigerated. Allow 30 minutes for the chutney to come to room temperature before serving.

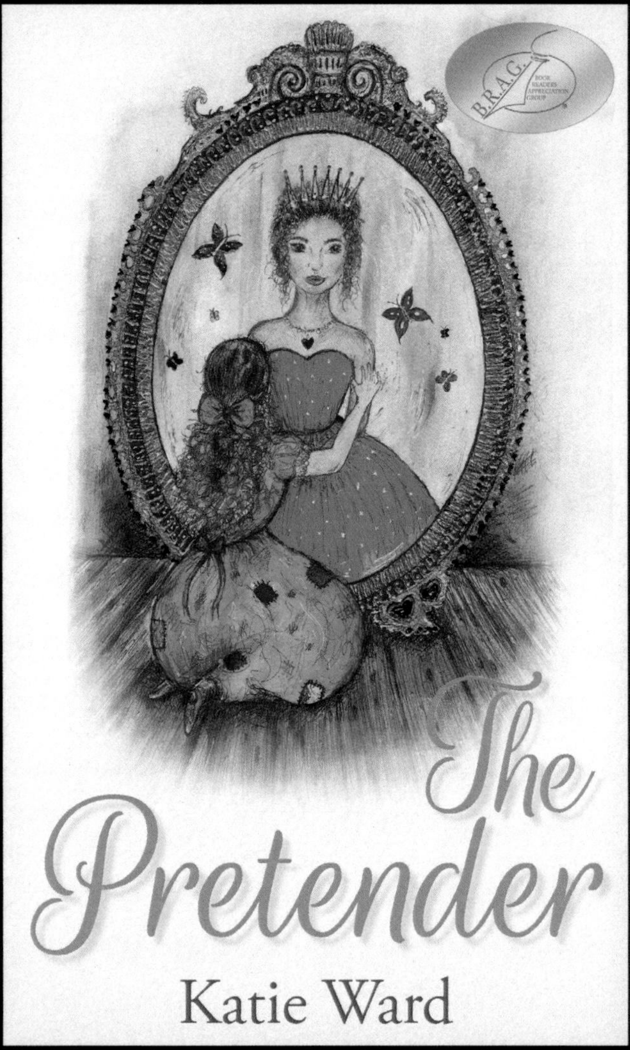

The Pretender

Named for the town in which it was invented in the 1930s, Coulommiers is a cow's milk cheese with the same buttery texture as Brie or Camembert. Once baked it is shared as tapas with crackers, bread or vegetable sticks. This is commonly eaten over drinks with friends. You can also serve individual portions with salad as a starter.

Life for Princess Isabella is far from a dream, trapped by tradition, protocol and the stifling burden of inheriting the crown; she longs to escape her shackles. After fleeing her abusive home, Sophia and Isabella meet at the palace gates. Realising how alike they look, they plan to switch places for one week. What could possibly go wrong? What starts out as a naïve plan to follow their dreams soon takes an unexpected turn with events quickly spiraling out of control. As the nightmare continues around them, it's a race against time to stem the devastating consequences of their actions.

www.katiewardwriter.com

Baked Coulommiers

For 4 people

INGREDIENTS

1 Coulommiers (usually 500g)
2 tbsp pine nuts
1 tsp rosemary
1 garlic clove
1 small onion
1 tsp honey
1 tbsp white wine
1 tbsp butter
salt and pepper

DIRECTIONS

1. Peel and chop the onion, peel and crush the garlic and remove the top skin of the Coulommiers with a knife.
2. Preheat oven to 390F. Melt the butter in a saucepan and cook the onion in it. When it takes on a golden color add the crushed garlic, salt, pepper, rosemary and honey. Stir well. When the honey is melted add the wine. Stir until there's no more liquid left at the bottom of the pan.
3. Place the Coulommiers in the middle of a sheet of tin foil or in a small oven dish. Top it with the butter-and-onion mixture and sprinkle with pine nuts.
4. Fold the tin foil tightly over the cheese and bake for 30 minutes.
5. Serve immediately. Mind the steam when you open the tin foil.

Don't hesitate to adapt the recipe to your taste, or to whatever you have in your pantry. Walnuts, chives, cream… be creative when it comes to the toppings. Also, if you can't find a Coulommiers in your local store, a Camembert will be a good substitute.

Courtesy of The Skinny French Chick

Mystery Genre

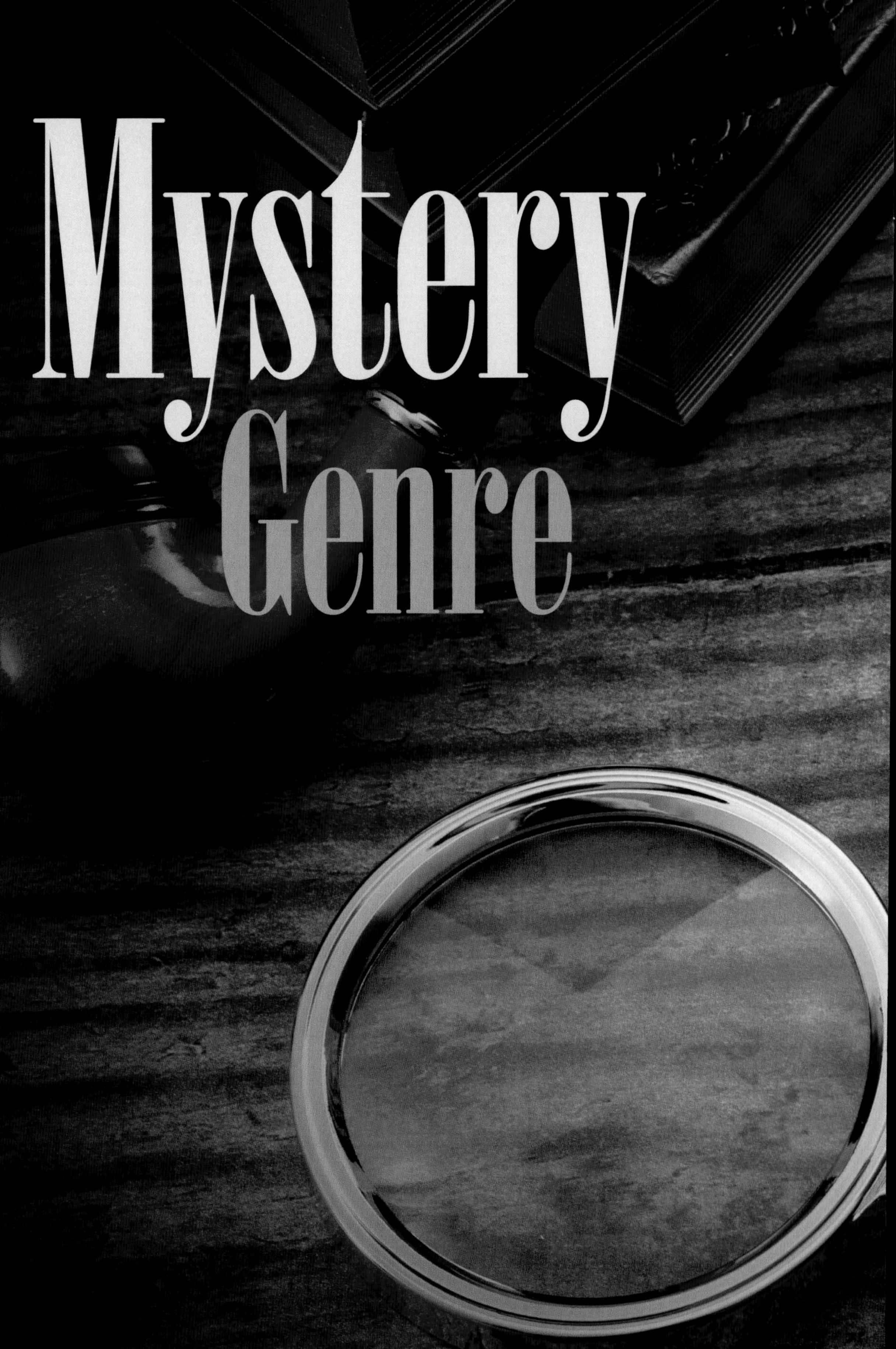

Betrayal
Quinoa, Bean, Corn and Pepper Salad

Curse Breaker
Mandarin Orange salad with
Raspberry Vinaigrette

Deadly Affair
Elegant Asparagus Soup

Death by Times New Roman
New York Cheesecake

Hush Girl: It's Only a Dream
Orange Glazed Sweet Rolls

Peggy Pinch, Policeman's Wife
Bubble and Squeak

The Lover's Portrait
Dutch apple Tart

Vain Pursuits
Osso Bucco

Betrayal

Betrayal is a timeslip mystery taking you from Modern day Saint John, New Brunswick, Canada to the Court of Henry VIII and Devon England. Modern day Lydia Hamilton loves Mexican food – not traditionally Atlantic Coast Canadian fare but her favorite just the same!

Betrayal tells the story, in alternating chapters of two women separated by time and place. Lydia Hamilton lives in modern day Canada, while Elisabeth Beeton lives in sixteenth century England. Lydia is living a perfect life, with her best friend and lover Dan Taylor, a family doctor. That is, until the nightmares start. Lydia becomes irrational while Dan worries about her sanity. He is deaf to her pleas that her dream state is in the guise of Elisabeth Beeton, a maid servant of Anne Boleyn. Dan can only see his perfect life drain away as he fights against Lydia's manic desire to find the woman of her dreams.

www.michelefkallio.com

Quinoa, Bean, Corn and Pepper Salad

Serves 6

INGREDIENTS

Vegetables

1 cup quinoa

1 15 oz can black beans or 1 ¾ cups homemade, rinsed and drained

1 cup cherry tomatoes, halved

1 cup fresh corn kernels

½ red bell pepper, deseeded and chopped

1 leek, chopped including green sections

2 tbsp red onion, chopped

2 tbsp chopped fresh parsley

Dressing

6 tbsp olive oil

5 tbsp lemon juice

1 tsp cumin

1 tsp salt

½ tsp pepper

DIRECTIONS

1. Cook quinoa according to package directions. Drain.
2. Place quinoa in a bowl and fluff with a fork. Add beans, tomatoes, corn, bell pepper, leek, red onions and parsley.
3. Dressing: Combine olive oil, lemon juice, and cumin. Whisk together and pour over vegetables. Season with salt and pepper.
4. Serve immediately or store in refrigerator until ready to eat.

Original recipe is vegan, gluten free and dairy free.

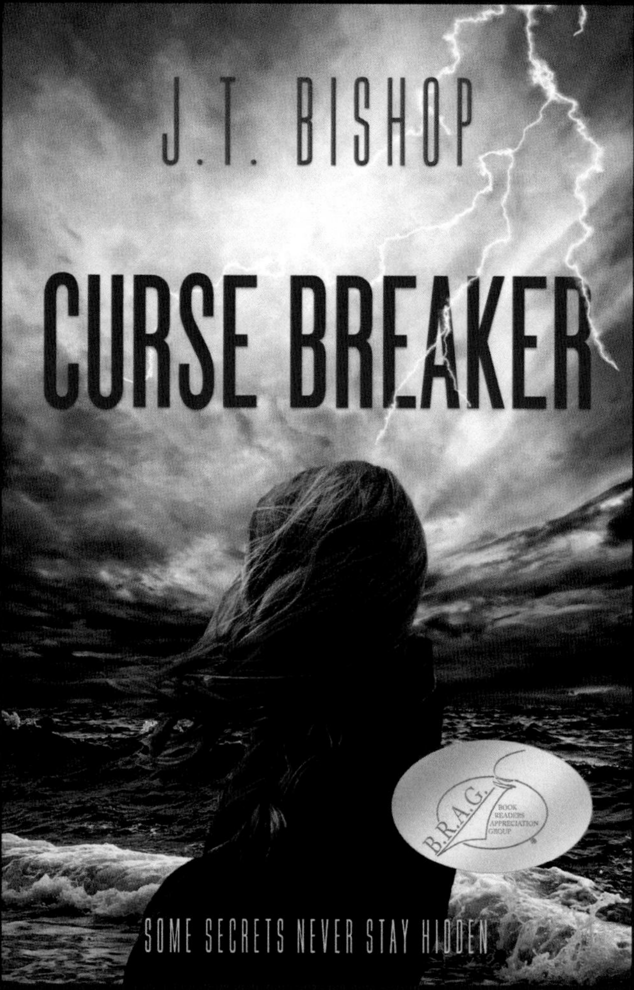

Curse Breaker

At the end of the meal, Gillian held her belly, exclaiming the food had been excellent. Grayson was pleased they had all managed to talk without any mention of death or curses.

From *Curse Breaker*

Grayson Steele is on the brink of suicide. The women he loves are dying. And he can't stop it.

Gillian Fletcher wants to help. She has a plan. Catch the killer who's making Grayson Steele's life a living hell. But there's only one way to do it. She has to be the bait.

As Grayson and Gillian's plan takes shape, they have no idea of the secrets that will be revealed. Secrets that will reveal not just a killer, but hidden truths that neither may be prepared to face.

Truths that will change their future forever.

Mandarin Orange Salad With Raspberry Vinaigrette

Serves 4-6

INGREDIENTS

Sugared Almonds
1 cup slivered almonds or pecans
2 tbsp sugar
1 head romaine lettuce, shredded
1 celery stalks, small dice
2 green onions, thinly sliced
1-11oz. can mandarin oranges, drain
Raspberry Vinaigrette
¼ cup sugar
¼ cup raspberry vinegar
2 tbsp fresh parsley, finely chopped
1 tsp salt
Dash black pepper
Dash cayenne
Dash Tabasco sauce
½ cup olive oil

Tip: If you can't find raspberry vinegar, use any white vinegar and add 2 tablespoons of raspberry jam, minus the sugar. Use sugar free jam if you want a sugar free recipe.

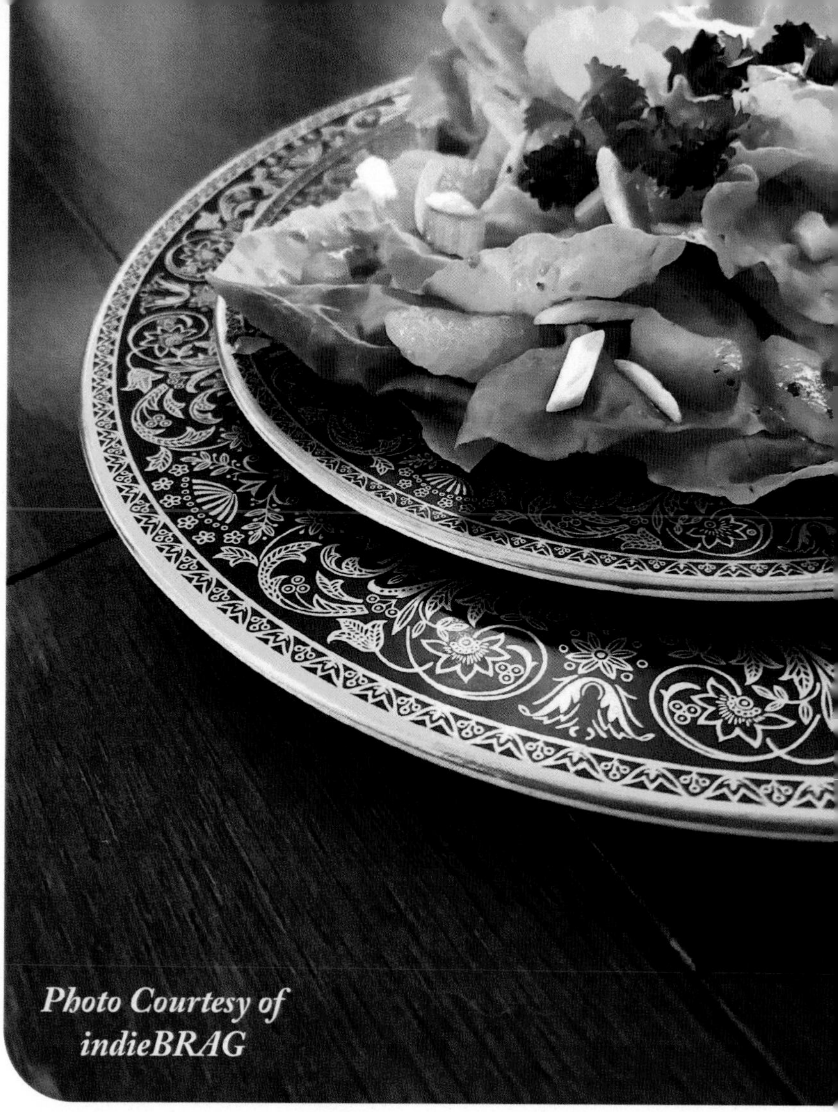

Photo Courtesy of indieBRAG

DIRECTIONS

Salad

1. 1 head Boston Bibb or Butter Lettuce, cut into bite size pieces
2. ½ small head of radicchio, shredded, optional

Sugared Almonds or Pecans

1. Stir sugar constantly in saucepan over low flame until sugar melts.
2. Add almonds. Cool and break apart.

Raspberry Vinaigrette

1. Mix first 7 ingredients together.
2. Add olive oil slowly, beating with a whisk or fork until the vinaigrette thickens.

Toss lettuces, celery, onions, mandarin oranges and almonds together with vinaigrette.

Serve and enjoy.

Autumn 1763. Career diplomat Alec Halsey has been elevated to a marquessate he doesn't want, and Polite Society believes he doesn't deserve. And with the suspicion he murdered his brother still lingering in London drawing rooms, returning to London after seven months in seclusion might well be a mistake. So, when a nobody vicar drops dead beside him at a party-political dinner, and his rabble-rousing uncle Plantagenet is bashed and left for dead in a laneway, Alec's foreboding deepens. Who would want a seemingly harmless man of God murdered, and why?

www.lucindabrant.com

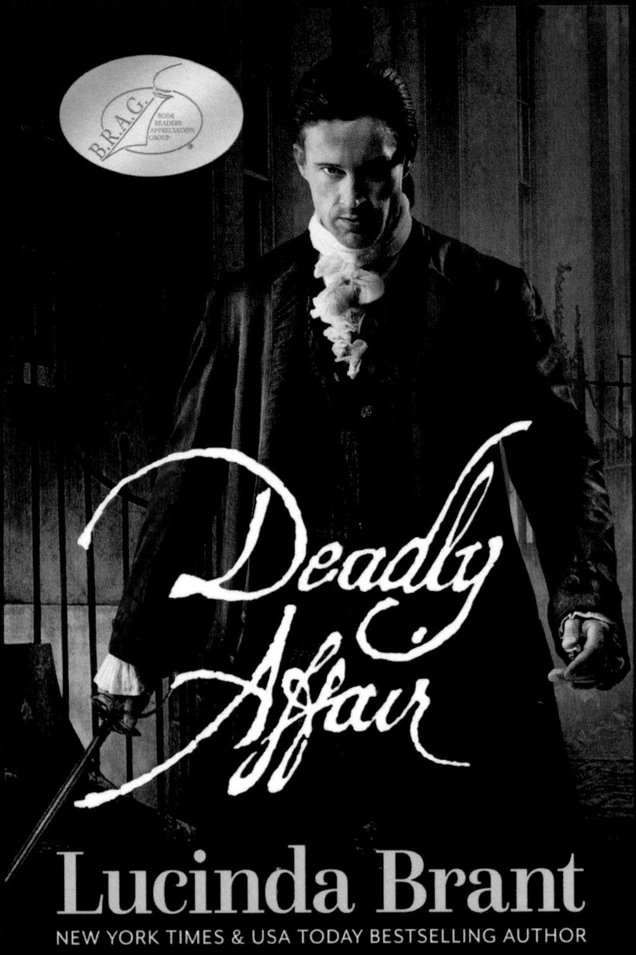

Deadly Affair

"A good hanging was one thing, but to witness a dinner guest dropping dead over the port... Well! It was unspeakably distasteful and downright bad-mannered."

From *A Deadly Affair*

Expandthetable Suggestions:

Make it creamy: Add ¼ cup heavy cream or half and half after soup has been puréed, stirring to combine thoroughly.

Make it heartier: Use chicken stock for a heartier taste.

Asparagus Soup

Serves 4

INGREDIENTS

2 lbs of asparagus
2 tbsp butter
2 shallots, chopped
1 clove garlic, minced
½ tsp salt
¼ tsp pepper
2 sprigs fresh thyme, leaves removed
4 cups vegetable stock

DIRECTIONS

1. Trim asparagus tough ends. Cut asparagus into 2-3" segments.
2. Melt butter in soup pot. Add shallots and garlic and cook over medium heat for 2 minutes, stirring so shallots and garlic do not burn.
3. Add asparagus, salt, pepper, thyme and stock.
4. Bring to a boil and then lower to a simmer for 15 minutes or until the asparagus is tender.
5. Cook a bit and then purée with an immerser or a blender until velvety smooth. Taste and adjust seasonings.
6. Serve with a few croutons or a sprig of thyme.

Death by Times New Roman

FBI Special Agent Cat Kavanagh dines in an elegant country club with best-selling mystery writer Bradley R. Woodbury- "His request for dinner included a soup course, an elegant spinach salad, the main entre of salmon stuffed with a pâté of scallops and cream cheese, a sorbet to cleanse the palate, and finally, homemade cheesecake."

From *Death by Times New Roman*

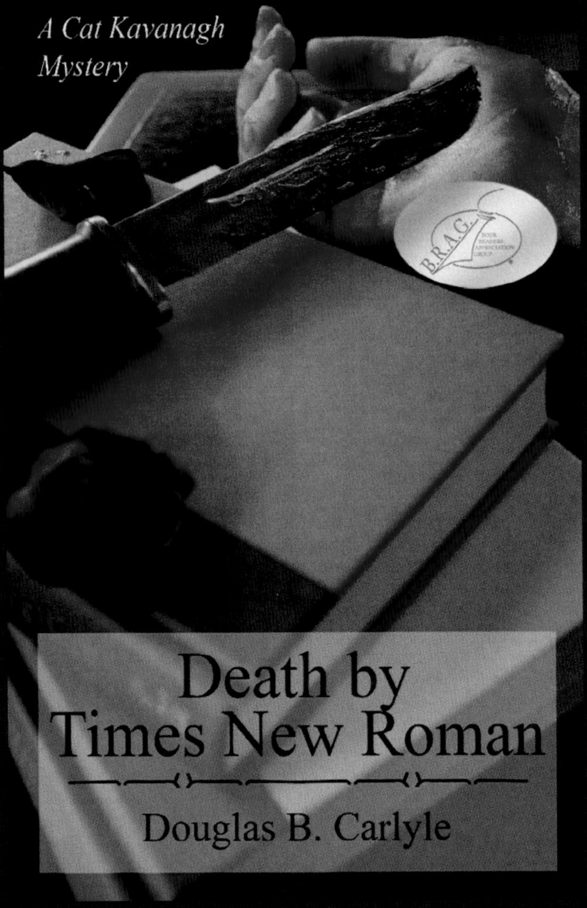

Eighteen books; eighteen towns; eighteen murders. FBI Special Agent Cat Kavanagh is trailing a vicious serial killer who stabs each of his victims in the heart, leaving behind the knife still embedded. It is more than coincidental that every time author Bradley R. Woodbury publishes another best-selling novel, police always find a dead woman in the same quiet town the author had chosen for his book. A decorated former Army Captain, Kavanagh is tough, cunning, and beautiful. Now, she is the bait for Woodbury's final novel. Will she find the killer before she, too, suffers Death by Times New Roman?

www.dbcarlyle.com

New York Cheesecake

INGREDIENTS

Crust:

1½ cups or 18 graham crackers
¼ cup butter
2 tbsp sugar

Cake:

4 eight-oz packages cream cheese, softened at room temperature
1½ cup sugar
5 eggs
1 tsp vanilla

DIRECTIONS

Crust:

1. Preheat oven to 325F.
2. Crush graham crackers. Melt butter and add sugar and mix with crushed graham crackers.
3. Spread graham cracker mixture on the bottom and sides of a 9" springform pan, pressing firmly and evenly. Bake for 10 minutes and remove from oven. Set aside while making the filling.

Cake:

1. Preheat oven to 350F. Using a mixer or by hand, cream the softened cream cheese. Add sugar and mix until creamy.
2. One at a time, add eggs into bowl, mixing well after each egg. Mix in vanilla.
3. Wrap bottom of spring form pan in aluminum foil. Pour the cheese mixture onto the crust. Place the wrapped pan in a large baking pan and place in oven.
4. Pour hot water carefully into the pan until the water comes halfway up the sides of the springform pan. Bake for about 1 hour and 15 minutes or until the edges of the cheesecake are golden and the center barely moves.
5. Remove cheesecake from water bath and oven and place on a rack to cool, for about 1 hour. Cover tightly with plastic wrap and place in refrigerator for 4-5 hours or overnight.

To serve: Release and remove the sides of the springform pan. Leave on the bottom of the pan. Place on a cake plate and refrigerate until you want to serve. Refrigerate leftovers.

To freeze: Cut into slices and wrap each piece in plastic wrap and then place in a freezer container or zip lock bag. Freezes well for 4-5 weeks.

Expandthetable Suggestions:

Chocolate Ganache: The ultimate for chocolate lovers. Ingredients: 9 oz chocolate, chopped, and 8 oz heavy cream. Heat cream over a medium heat until it is steamy but before it boils. Pour over chocolate and stir gently until chocolate is melted. Cool slightly and pour carefully over top of cheesecake, starting at center and working out to the edges. This makes a totally amazing presentation.

Hush Girl: It's Only a Dream

"Feeling like I needed something to go with the note I'd written for CC, I baked a pan of gooey, caramel, cinnamon rolls. In the years since Matt and I had married, I perfected a recipe I'd gotten from Matt's Uncle Tony".

From *Hush Girl*

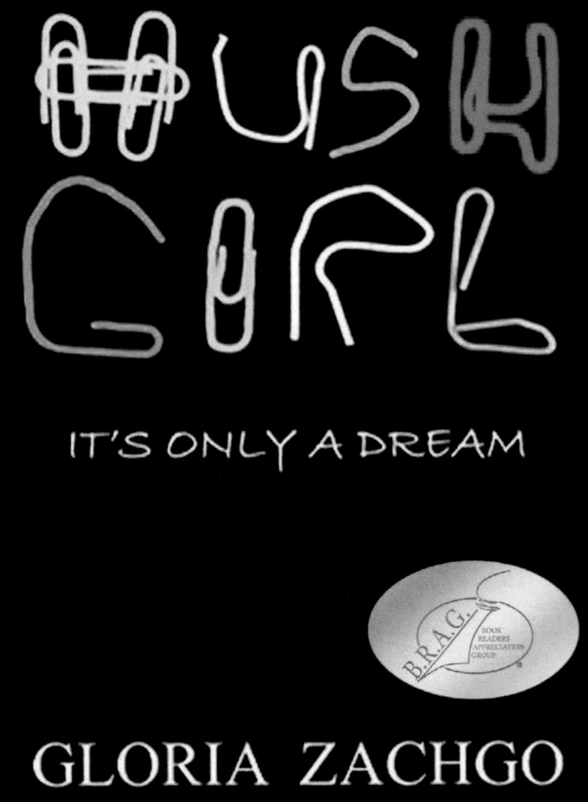

Hush Girl: It's Only a Dream were words that had always silenced Nicki as a child. She didn't understand the nightmares that continued to follow her into adulthood until she sought psychological help. As she started unraveling her painful past, someone from the present tried to keep her from remembering. But a family's hidden secrets were unsealed when she and her daughter's life were endangered. Nicki's story is a blended genre: mystery, thriller, suspense, and romance. It's a journey filled with pain, terror, healing, and redemption.

www.gloriazachgo.com

Glazed Orange Sweet Rolls

Photo Courtesy of Susan Weintrob

Yield 2 dozen

INGREDIENTS

2 cups all-purpose flour
1 package active dry yeast
1 cup milk
¼ cup sugar
¼ cup vegetable oil or butter, softened to room temperature
1 tsp salt
2 eggs
2 cups all-purpose flour
¼ cup butter
2 tsp cinnamon
¼ cup sugar
½ cup raisins, optional
½ cup chocolate chips, optional
¼ cup marmalade, melted
¼ cup confectioner's sugar dissolved in 1 tsp water

DIRECTIONS

1. In a large mixing bowl, combine 2 cups flour and the yeast. Warm the milk, sugar, oil and salt. Add to flour and yeast mixture. Add 2 eggs and stir to mix.
2. Beat at low speed with electric mixer for 1 minute. Beat 3 additional minutes at high speed or stir vigorously by hand.
3. By hand, stir in 2 cups flour to make a moderately stiff dough. Knead on lightly floured surface until smooth and elastic. Shape into a ball and place in a lightly greased bowl, turning to cover dough with the oil.
4. Cover with plastic wrap and place in a draft fee location and let rise until doubled, about 1 hour. To make later in day, place in refrigerator for a few hours or overnight, then bring to room temperature and let rise.
5. Punch down, divide in half and let rest for a few minutes.
6. Roll one half into a rectangle that is approximately 12" by 8". Brush dough with half the butter. Sprinkle with half the sugar and cinnamon. Add raisins and or chocolate chips if desired. Spread filling to one half inch of the edge of the dough.
7. Roll dough up starting with long side as for a jelly roll and seal seam with your fingers, adding a little water if needed. Repeat with the other piece of dough.
8. With a sharp knife, slice each piece about 12 times to make the rolls, about 1" each. Place rolls cut side down on a 9"by 1 ½" greased round baking pan, leaving a small space between each roll for rising. Let rise for 30 minutes or until double.
9. Bake at 375F for 15-18 minutes.
10. Drizzle with marmalade and or confectioner's sugar over warm rolls.

Adapted from *Homemade Bread Cook Book*, Better Homes and Garden

Peggy Pinch, Policeman's Wife, is the first of three detective novels set in 1920s rural England. Peggy has to negotiate a turbulent marriage to the village Constable Arthur Pinch and overcome many of the prejudices of her time. With the help of her best friend, a retired school ma'am, Peggy demonstrates a talent for solving murder cases while PC Pinch and his male colleagues are often left puzzled. Throughout, the books show a humorous and tongue-in-cheek view of village life in times gone by.

www.bookcabin.co.uk

Peggy Pinch, Policeman's Wife

Bubble and Squeak, named for the sound the cabbage makes while cooking, is from the 18th century, it was typically made with leftovers from the Sunday roast and eaten the next day. It is considered one of the most "British" foods and certainly Peggy would serve it to PC Pinch.

Bubble and Squeak

Serves 4

INGREDIENTS

4 tbsp oil
2 lbs potatoes, mashed
1 medium carrot, diced
1 small bunch broccoli, chopped
½ cup onion, chopped
2 cups cabbage, sliced thinly or chopped
2 eggs, beaten

DIRECTIONS

1. Steam carrots and broccoli. Drain and set aside.
2. In frying pan, warm 2 tablespoon oil over medium heat. Add onion and sauté until translucent. Add cabbage (and the rest of any uncooked vegetables you may be using) and sauté until soft. Put mashed potatoes into bowl and mix together with cooked vegetables. Add eggs and mix together.
3. Add remaining 2 tablespoons oil into pan. Place potato mixture into pan and press down gently with spatula to make even. Or you may make the mixture into patties, the size of your choice.
4. Continue to fry in pan until golden on bottom, adding oil as needed. Flip and continue cooking until bottom side is browned.
5. You may also place the mixture in an ovenproof pan into a 400F preheated oven. Flip after bottom is browned, about 10-12 minutes. Cook an additional 10 minutes or until top is browned.

Tip: Flipping is tricky if you are making the Bubble and Squeak as one large dish. Use a sturdy plate or cutting board to flip and then slide back carefully into pan.

Expandthetable Suggestions:
Add a poached or sunny side up eggs up on top

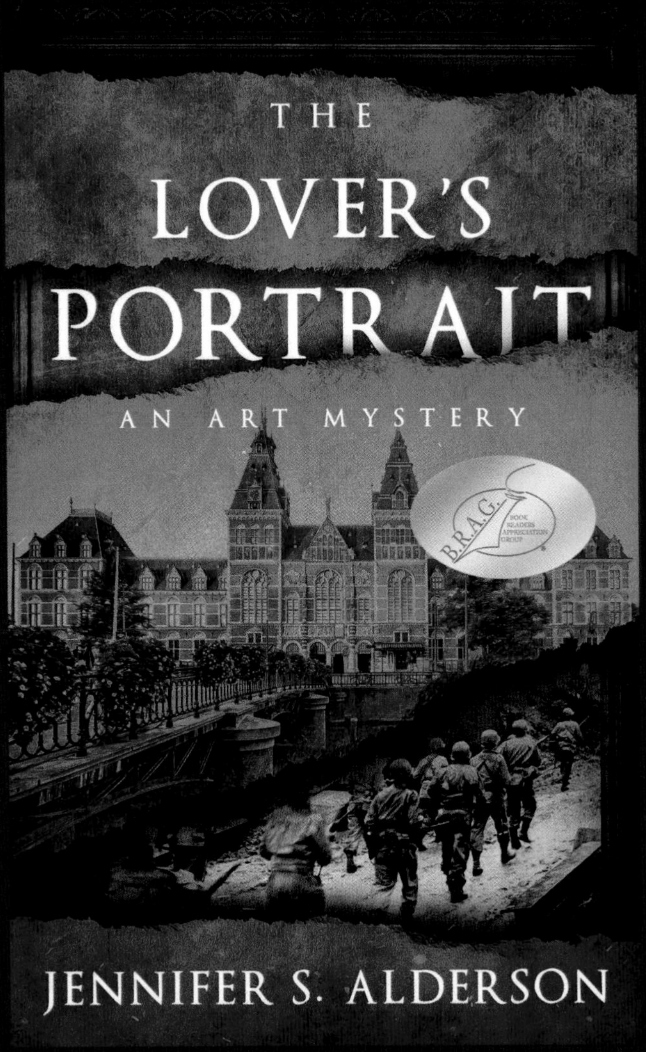

The Lover's Portrait

Cafes abound throughout the Netherlands and Zelda and Frederich visit many for some wonderful coffee. A traditional accompaniment to the coffee is the Dutch Apple Tart, a very delicious piling of apples in a sweet crust. Cut yourself a slice and sip some coffee as you read all about Zelda's adventures!

Museum intern Zelda Richardson is swept into the mystery surrounding artwork hidden from the Nazis. A portrait holds the key to recovering a cache of looted artwork, secreted away during World War II. But Zelda's not the only one searching for the missing paintings — and her rival would kill to find them first...

A captivating historical art thriller set in the 1940s and present-day Amsterdam.

www.jennifersalderson.com

Dutch Apple Tart

Serves 8

INGREDIENTS

Pastry
½ cup white sugar
½ cup brown sugar
1 cup butter, softened
3 cups all-purpose flour
½ tsp salt
1 tsp cinnamon
1 tbsp finely ground bread crumbs
2 eggs beaten for dough
1 egg beaten for egg wash
2 tbsp melted marmalade
Filling
3 lbs tart apples, peeled, cored and sliced
½ cup golden raisins
2 tbsp Grand Marnier or Amaretto
¼ cup white sugar
1 tbsp cinnamon

DIRECTIONS

1. Spray a 10"spring form pan and set aside.
2. In a bowl, cream sugars and butter. Add 2 eggs. Combine flour, salt, and cinnamon. Add to sugar mixture and stir. Knead by hand on a lightly floured surface until smooth.
3. Roll out three quarters of dough into a 11" circle. Press over bottom and sides of pan. Sprinkle the breadcrumbs evenly over the dough.
4. Preheat oven to 350F.
5. Soak raisins in liqueur for 10 minutes or so until raisins are plumped. Drain.
6. Mix apples, raisins, sugar and cinnamon. Attractively arrange apples over dough.
7. Rollout remaining dough in a circle. Cut strips about ½ to ⅓" wide. With the 2 longest strips, make an X in the center of the tart. Create a lattice by weaving vertical and horizontal strips in an over and under pattern, trimming excess dough.
8. Brush egg wash over lattice. Bake in preheated oven for about 60 minutes or until apples are soft and pastry is golden. Remove from oven. Brush melted marmalade over lattice strips. Cool before serving.

This second book in the Bunny Elder series finds Bunny flying off to romantic Italy as traveling companion to her newly widowed sister, Dolly Parton look-alike, Linda. She never suspects this shopping trip to add a Neapolitan nativity set to her sister's collection will lead not only to pasta and pizza, but to peril, too.

https://jbhawker.wordpress.com/

Vain Pursuits

Bunny and her sister go on the trip of a lifetime! No Mystery set in the romantic country of Italy would be complete without some delicious Italian food!

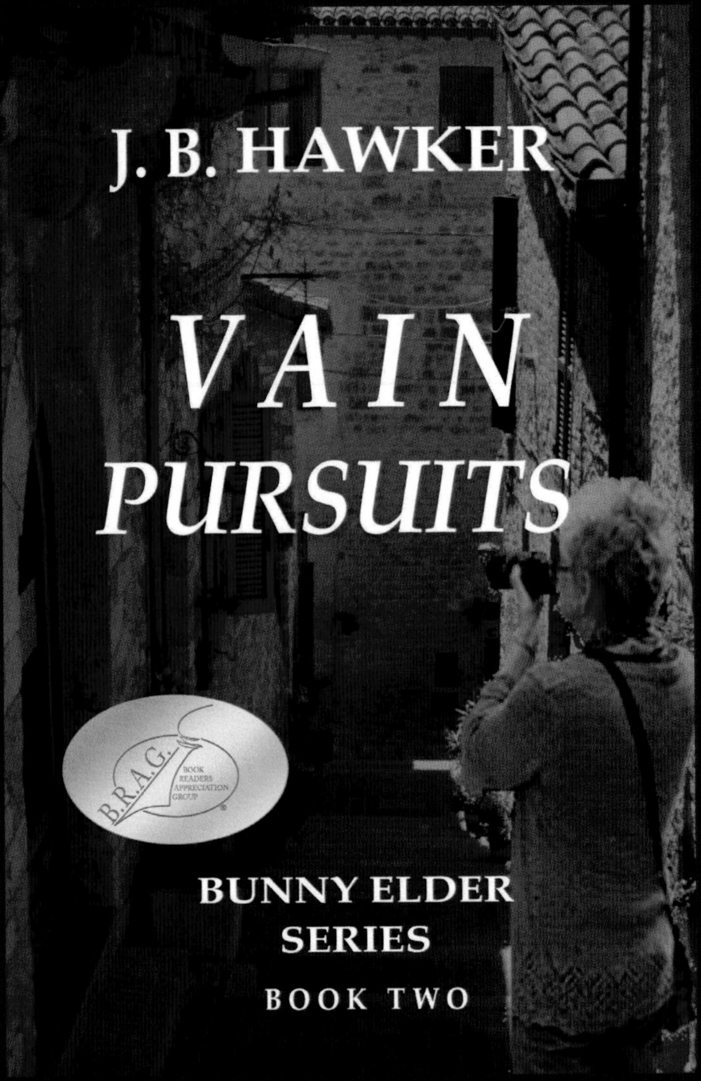

Osso Bucco

Serves 6 to 8

INGREDIENTS

6 tbsp butter
1 cup diced carrots
2 tsps finely chopped garlic
Salt
Flour
1 cup dry white wine
1 bouquet garnie*
1 tsp dried thyme
parsley
bay leaves (2)
1 ½ cups finely chopped onion
1 cup diced celery
6 to 8 pounds veal shank
Freshly ground black pepper
¾ cup olive oil
1 tsp dried basil
1 cup beef stock
1 35 oz. can chopped tomatoes

*To Make a Bouquet Garnie
Place herbs in a square of
cheesecloth ties with twine.

Traditional Herbs:

Fresh parsley
Thyme sprigs
Bay leaves
May also add:
Rosemary
Peppercorns
Tarragon
Basil
chervil

DIRECTIONS

1. Chop the onion, carrots, celery and garlic
2. In a large, heavy oven proof casserole or pot that has a tight cover, melt half of the butter (3 tablespoons) and ¼ cup of the olive oil over medium heat. Sautee the vegetables until translucent, remove from pan and set aside.
3. Season the pieces of veal with salt and pepper, then roll them in flour and shake off the excess. Heat the remaining olive oil and butter until a haze forms over it. Brown the veal 4 pieces at a time over moderately high heat, adding more oil or butter as needed. Transfer the browned pieces to a plate and set aside.
4. Preheat the oven to 350F. Discard some of the fat from the pan, leaving a film on the bottom. Pour in the wine and boil it briskly over high heat until it reduces. Scrape in any browned bits clinging to the pan. Stir in beef stock, basil, thyme, tomatoes, parsley, bay leaves, salt, pepper and bouquet garnie and bring to a boil.
5. Add vegetables to pot and simmer for 5 minutes. Add veal to pan. The liquid should at least come halfway up the sides of the veal and can even cover it if you have enough. If not, add more stock. Bring to a boil on top of stove. Turn off heat and taste for seasonings. Adjust as necessary.
6. Cover pan and transfer to oven. Bake in lower third of the oven and continue to check to make sure it is simmering gently. Remove from oven after 1 ½ hours. Veal should be very tender and should pierce easily with a knife.
7. Serve over pasta or egg noodles.

NON-FICTION GENRE

Common Questions Children Ask About Puberty

Family Taco Night

Feasible Planet

Beanie Burgers

Mother's Milks

Kitchari

Mulligan Stew

Mulligan Stew

Save Yourself

Lentil and Cabbage Soup

The Altitude Journals

Tibetan Noodle soup

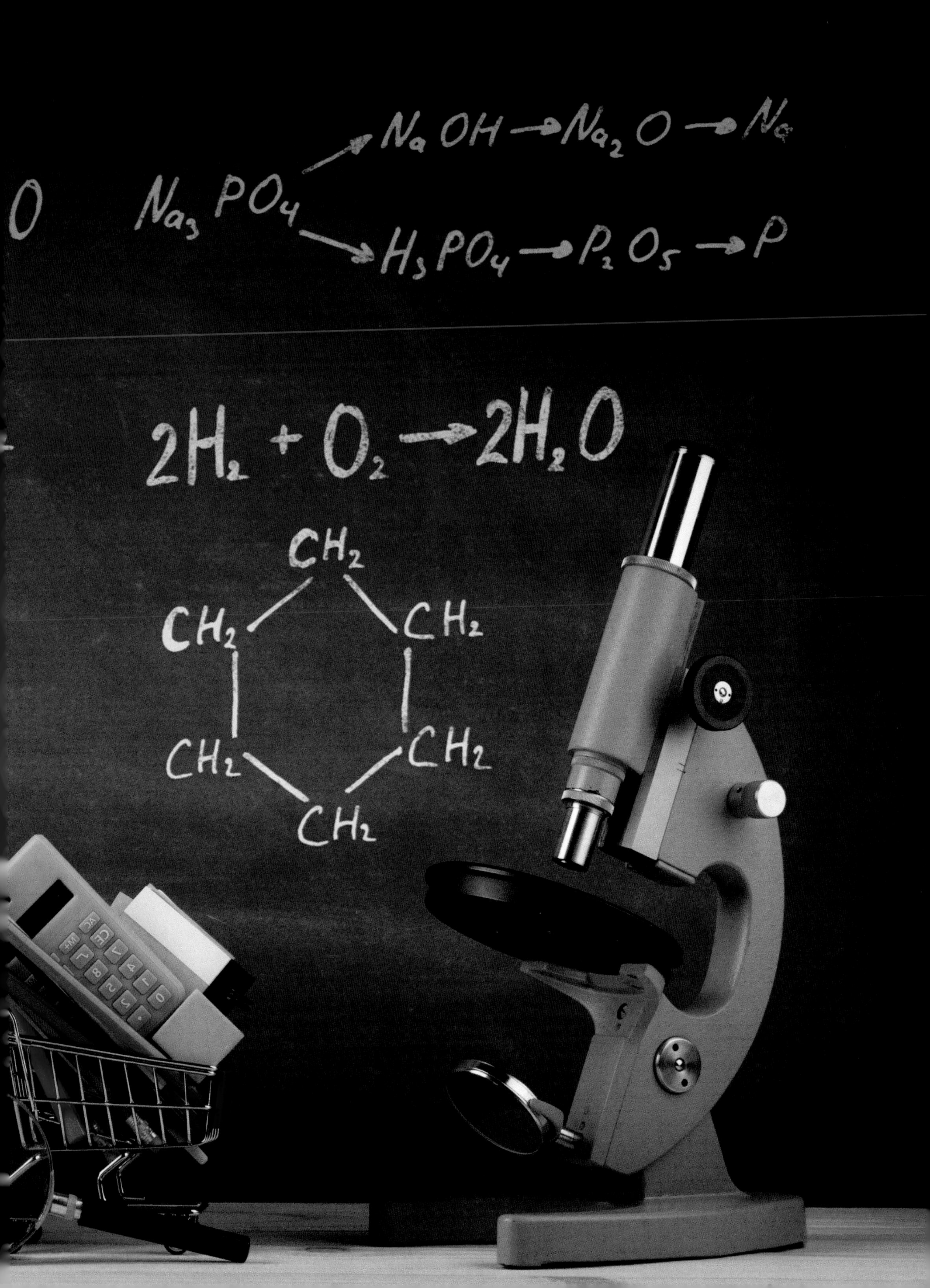

Na OH → Na2 O → Na
Na3 PO4
H3 PO4 → P2 O5 → P
2H2 + O2 → 2H2O
CH2
CH2
CH2
CH2
CH2
CH2

Common Questions Children Ask About Puberty

There is no doubt that making food together is a great activity for families and a way to bond with children. What could be better than a family taco night?

Imagine you are a nine-year-old child. You are growing hair in new places, feel weird, and notice your friends are beginning to smell. You have lots of questions about these occurrences and wish to have a trusted resource that can provide simple and honest answers. Now, imagine being an adult and a child starts asking you questions about these experiences. Do you know what to say? Do you know how to provide age-appropriate answers?

This book provides simple answers to basic questions people of all ages wonder about, as well as recommendations and discussion cards to help begin conversations.

www.pubertyprof.com

Family Taco Night

INGREDIENTS

Vegan

Lettuce, shredded
Spinach leaves
Tomatoes chopped
Cucumbers, chopped (peel if not organic)
Mushrooms, fresh or sautéed
Zucchini, shredded
Bell peppers, sliced
Radishes, thinly sliced
Onions, caramelized
Yellow or red onions, sliced
Jalapeño peppers, thinly sliced
Refried beans
Corn cut from cob
Roasted cauliflower florets
Tofu, cubed and crisply fried or baked

Vegetarian

Cheddar cheese, grated
Scrambled eggs

Meat

Chicken, beef, or pork, shredded

Fish

Breaded and baked cod pieces

Toppings

1 Avocado, sliced
Guacamole
2 scallions, diced
Olives, mixed and chopped
Salsa, how sweet or hot-- to your taste!
Sour cream with chopped scallions
Sliced lemons or limes

DIRECTIONS

Place taco on a plate and add a few of the choices above. Top with your favorite topping.

Expandthetable Suggestions:

Burritos: Add your choices to a burrito. Fold in sides and roll tightly.

Fajitas, Burrito cups or Pita: Fill with your choices.

Italian/French Bread: Instead of a taco, pile your choices on a long slice of Italian bread slightly hollowed out. Cut into 4-5" pieces for ease of eating

"Sustainable living means we need to be informed, vote smart, lobby hard, and to take personal action. For those who feel we could do more, this book is for you and is loaded with easy actionable activities, the reasons for doing them, and explores why we are not doing them already. Every journey start with a first step. Hopefully this book will lead you to take those first steps that will change the world!"

www.feasibleplanet.com

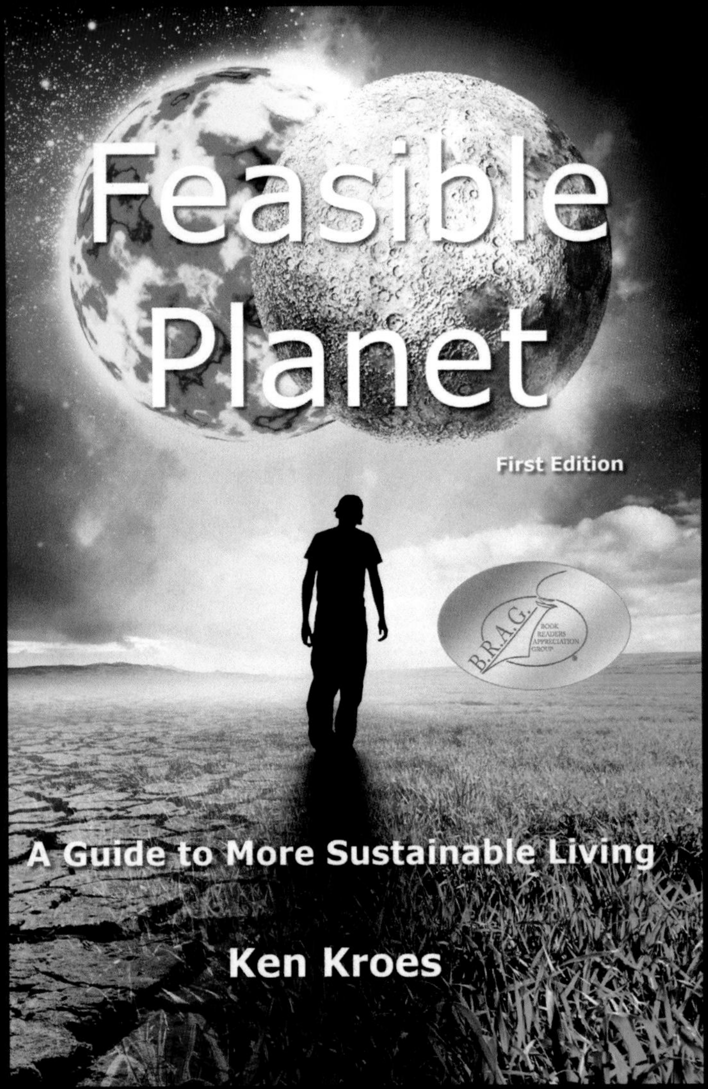

Feasible Planet

"Having meat in our diet is not a bad thing, but too much can be hard on the planet. Switching things up a bit and having a vegan meal a few times per week will not only add variety to your diet, but also reduce your carbon footprint and save you money at the same time."

From *Feasible Planet*

Beanie Burgers

Yield 5 burgers

INGREDIENTS

3 cups beans
¼ cup onion
1 egg
1 tbsp cumin
1 tbsp coriander
½ tsp salt
¼ tsp pepper
2-3 tbsp oil or butter if sautéing
½ cup quick oats, breadcrumbs or cornmeal
1 bun per burger

DIRECTIONS

1. Preheat oven to 350F.
2. Line a sheet tray with parchment paper.
3. Mash beans and onions by hand, in a blender or food processor, until desired consistency. Add seasoning and mix or blend for a few seconds. Put mixture into a bowl.
4. Form into 5 burgers, rolling in oats or breadcrumbs to hold together. Refrigerate for ½ hour or longer before cooking.
5. Bake at 350F for 15 minutes or sauté in frying pan in oil or butter. Cool and freeze at this stage if desired.
6. Serve on buns with coleslaw or avocado, sliced cucumber and bean sprouts.

Mother's Milks

This recipe is a tribute to all health traditions and their deep knowledge of the body.

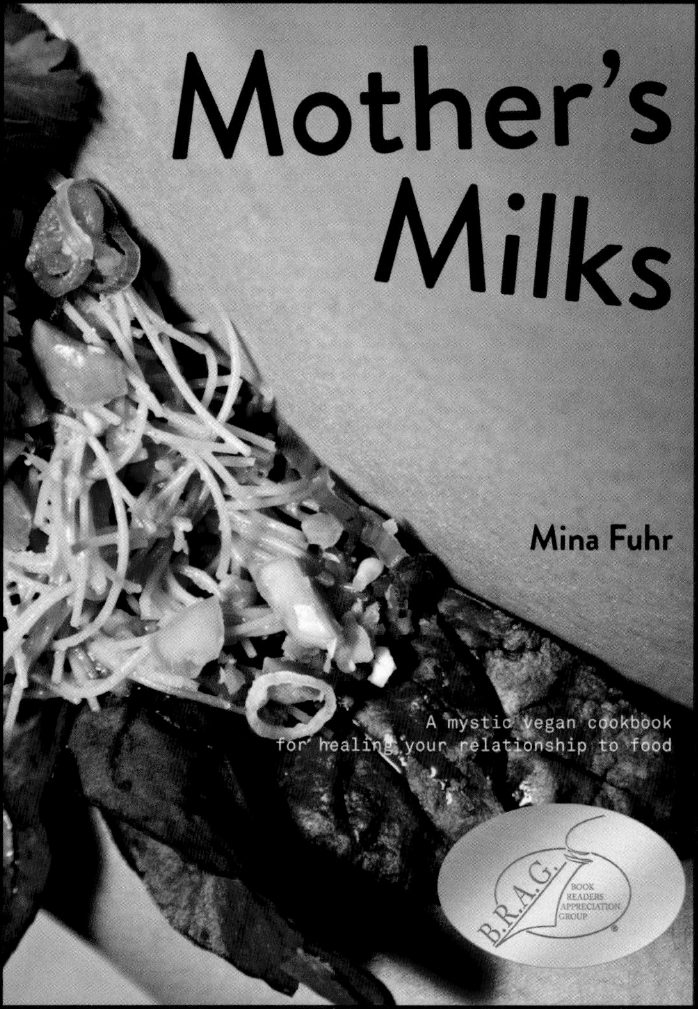

"Mother's Milks tells the story of Mina Fuhr's healing from her eating disorder with a courage and humility that is inspiring. Through Mina, the universe has birthed a glorious explosion of sensual recipes for healing. The book is a beautiful and powerful presence in the home. The food looks delicious. The photos come alive off the page. Simple and loving, each recipe, a manifestation of a virtue, speaks in tongues with a variety of flavors diverse enough to hook any taster into a dialogue with the idea of raw vegan nourishment.

www.minalange.com

Kitchari Doodle Do

INGREDIENTS

½ cup rice
½ cup mung beans
½ tbsp ghee or coconut oil
½ tsp coriander
½ tsp cumin
½ tsp turmeric
½ tsp pepper
2 cardamom pods
2 cloves garlic chopped
1 tbsp chopped ginger
½ tsp salt

Topping

½ onion
½ cup raspberries
2 tbsp olive oil
1 tbsp lemon juice
salt & pepper to taste
handful of arugula

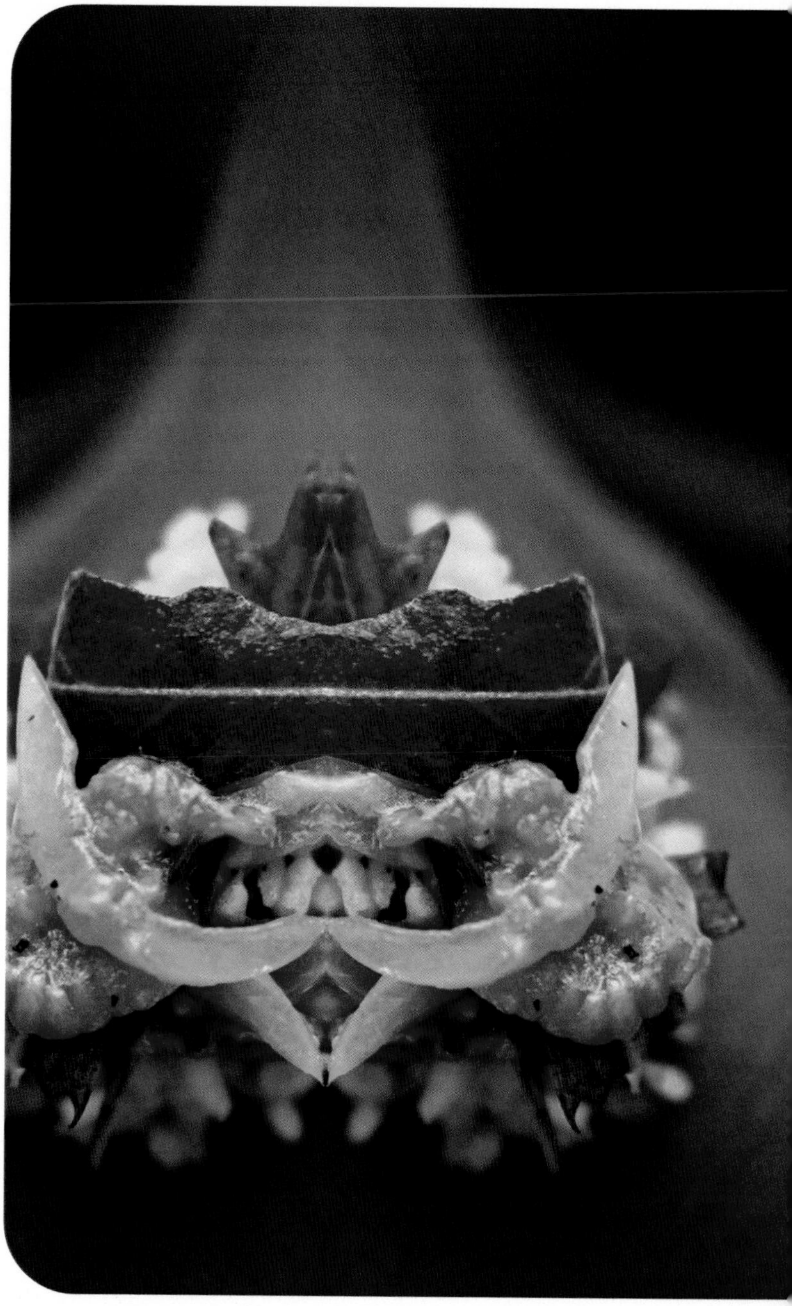

DIRECTIONS

1. Soak the rice and mung beans in water overnight.
2. In a saucepan, heat the ghee and add the spices, then stir for 30 seconds. Add the rinsed rice and mung beans, stirring again for 30 seconds.
3. Add a cup of water, cover, and let simmer until all liquid is absorbed. Turn off the heat and let it sit for another 5 min.

Topping

Thinly slice the onion. Put all ingredients in a bowl and mix gently with your hands until everything is well combined. Serve the kitchari with a generous amount of the topping.

Recipe and photo Courtesy of Mina Fuhr

Mulligan Stew contains a variety of ingredients from the hobo culture: hobo life as it was lived at the turn of the twentieth century, women hobos, hobo heroes, hobo signs and symbols, contemporary hobos telling of their experiences, and hobo traditions from the National Hobo Convention in Britt, Iowa—an event that has opened a door into the hobo world every August for more than 100 years. The convention motto is "There's a Little Bit of Hobo in All of Us." Readers who are hobos at heart are invited to open this book and savor the stew.

www.writersuncorked.wordpress.com

Mulligan Stew

Nothing speaks more to the American Hobo culture more than a hearty Mulligan Stew!

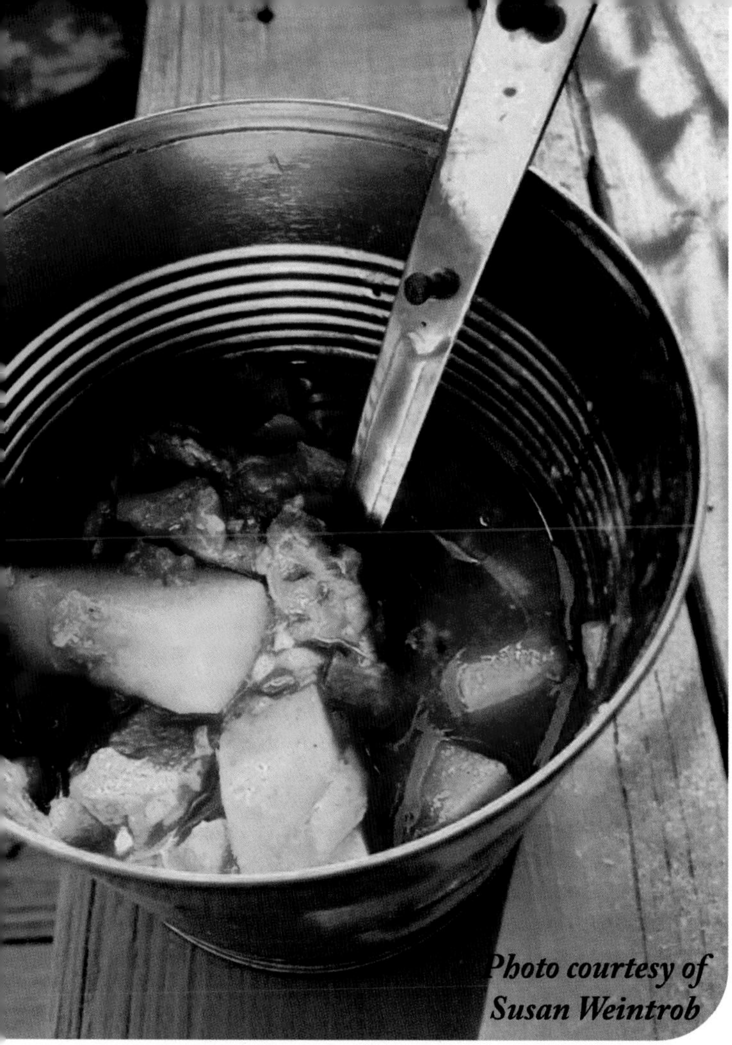
Photo courtesy of Susan Weintrob

Mulligan Stew

INGREDIENTS

1 lb stewing beef, cubed
2 tbsp flour
2-3 tbsp olive oil
2 onions, chopped
1 garlic clove, minced
2 medium carrots, chopped
1 lb small potatoes or larger ones chopped
2 sprigs thyme or ½ tsp dried
1 cup red wine or 1 bottle of beer
14.5 oz diced tomatoes canned
1 tsp white or brown sugar or ½ tsp sugar substitute
1 tsp salt,
1 tsp pepper

DIRECTIONS

1. Take cubed beef and marinate in balsamic vinegar for 2 hours or longer. This is helpful for slightly tougher cuts of beef.
2. In heavy pan over medium heat, heat olive oil. Drain and reserve liquid. Add cubed beef and sprinkle flour over the beef. Stir to combine. Cook about 3-4 minutes, or until beef cubes are browned. Remove and set aside.
3. Add onions, garlic, carrots, potatoes and thyme sautéing gently for about 10 minutes. Add more oil if necessary.
4. Add back beef cubes and reserved liquid to vegetables, along with canned tomatoes, wine or beer, sugar, salt and pepper. Bring to a boil and then lower heat to a simmer.
5. Cover and cook for 1 ½ to 2 hours or until beef is tender. Salt and pepper to taste.

Notes:

As this is an improvised stew, feel free to add vegetables on hand—turnips, parsnips, mushrooms, peas and so on. While fresh is always better, use canned or frozen when needed. Use about 3 pounds of vegetables.

Drain before sautéing and do not add back into mixture.

After Step 4, you may also cook the stew in a 325F oven for 2 hours or until beef is tender.

Lentil-Cabbage Soup

Yield 6 cups

INGREDIENTS

½ cup onion, diced
1 tbsp olive oil
2 cups cooked lentils
3 carrots, diced
2 cups shredded and chopped cabbage
Large handful kale, chopped
4 cups water or stock
¼ cup tomato sauce
½ tbsp oregano, dried
½ tsp basil, dried
½ tsp thyme, dried
1 tsp salt
¼ tsp pepper

DIRECTIONS

1. In a large pot, add onions and olive oil. Sauté onions until softened. Add rest of ingredients and bring to a boil.
2. Reduce heat to medium, simmer for 20-25 minutes or until vegetables are soft. Taste and adjust seasoning.

The Altitude Journals

Tibet's people, it's culture and of course, Mount Everest play a big part in David Mauro's journey.

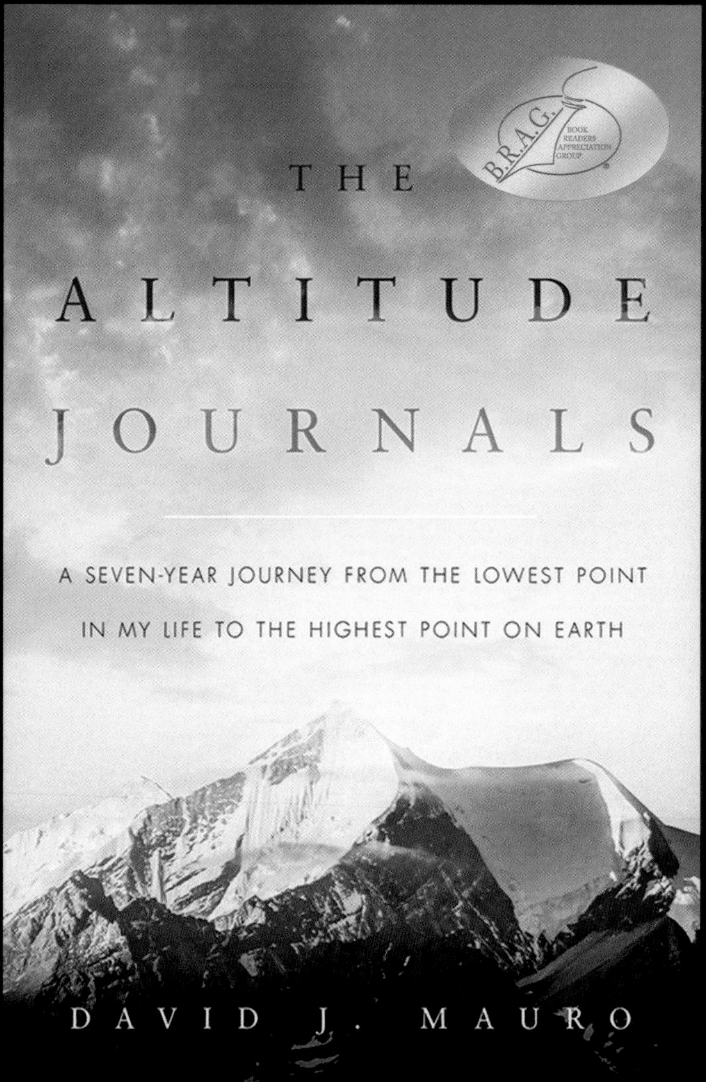

When David Mauro was in his forties, his life hit rock bottom. With nothing to lose, he left everything he knew behind and set out on an epic adventure. For the next seven years, Dave trudged across glaciers, frozen wastelands and through dense, dangerous forests. He communed with penguins and elephants, kept company with cannibals and gunrunners, and spoke with the dead. And though he'd never been a climber, he ended up joining history's courageous few when he ascended into the clouds to stand at the summit of Mount Everest.

The Altitude Journal is the poignant, inspiring, and exciting true story of a remarkable midlife crisis.

www.davidjmauro.com

Tibetan Noodle Soup (Thukpa)

Serves 2-3

INGREDIENTS

2-3 tbsp sesame oil
2 shallots, chopped
3 garlic cloves, minced
1 tsp chopped ginger
1 tsp coriander
1 tsp cumin
1 tsp turmeric
1 medium carrot, cut into matchsticks
3 tomatoes chopped
4-5 cups vegetable stock
1 tbsp soy sauce
Rice noodles
Chopped green onion for garnish

DIRECTIONS

1. Warm sesame oil in soup pot. Add shallots and garlic and cook 2-3 minutes until softened.
2. Add ginger, coriander, cumin and turmeric. Stir to combine.
3. Add carrots, tomatoes and stock. Bring to boil and then cover and lower to a simmer for 5 minutes.
4. While simmering, cook rice noodles according to the package directions. Drain noodles and add to soup.
5. Garnish with chopped green onion.

Expandthetable Suggestions:

Add cubed tofu to soup with carrots and tomatoes.

Add cooked shredded beef or chicken with the carrots and tomatoes.

Romance Genre

A.K.A.
Guinness Chili with Beans

A Newfound Land
Christmas Saffron Buns

Been Searching For You
Savory Stuffed Mushrooms

Davinia's Duke
Yorkshire Cakes

Eva's Secret
Moroccan Stew

Flux
Cauliflower & Potato Salad

The Things We Don't Say
Ranger Cookies

A.K.A.

Morgan works in a pub in Oregon. Traditional "Pub Grub" includes many of the English favorites but has expanded around the world to include burgers, chicken wings and Morgan's favorite - Chili!

Would you give up everything for justice? Morgan Steel is a rising-star ADA from LA. When her half-sister is brutally murdered her world spins off course, tilts off its axis. Seeking justice, she commits the unthinkable and finds herself no longer living in a world of right or wrong, black or white. It is a reality within a false reality of love, lust, betrayal, and murder.

www.tlalexanderauthor.com

Guinness Chili with Vegetables and Bean

Serves 16

INGREDIENTS

2 tbsp olive oil
1 large onion, medium dice
2 bell peppers, medium dice
8 stalks celery, medium dice
4 carrots, medium dice
1 zucchini, medium dice
2 cups dry black beans
1 cup dry black-eyed peas
1 28-oz can diced tomatoes
1 28-oz can of tomato purée
4 cups stock or water
1 can Guinness Beer

Spice blend

1 tbsp brown sugar
1 tbsp ground coriander
1 tbsp ground cumin
2 tsp chili powder
1 tsp salt
¼ tsp black pepper
¼ tsp cinnamon

DIRECTIONS

1. Heat the oil in a large pot on medium high heat and add all the vegetables.
2. Sautee for 10-15 minutes to soften.
3. Add beans, diced tomato and tomato puree. Stir until combined.
4. Add stock or water, Guinness and all spices. Mix well and bring to a boil.
5. Then, reduce heat to medium low and cook, covered for about 4 hours or until beans are tender. Stir every 30 minutes or so. If chili looks too thick, add water a little at a time until you have reached the desired consistency.
6. Eat as is or serve over rice, mashed potatoes, baked potato or grain of choice.
7. Serve with a dollop of sour cream or grated cheese if desired.

A Newfound Land

Anna Belfrage is a wonderful writer and cook! Christmas Saffron Buns are a tradition in Sweden and loved everywhere!

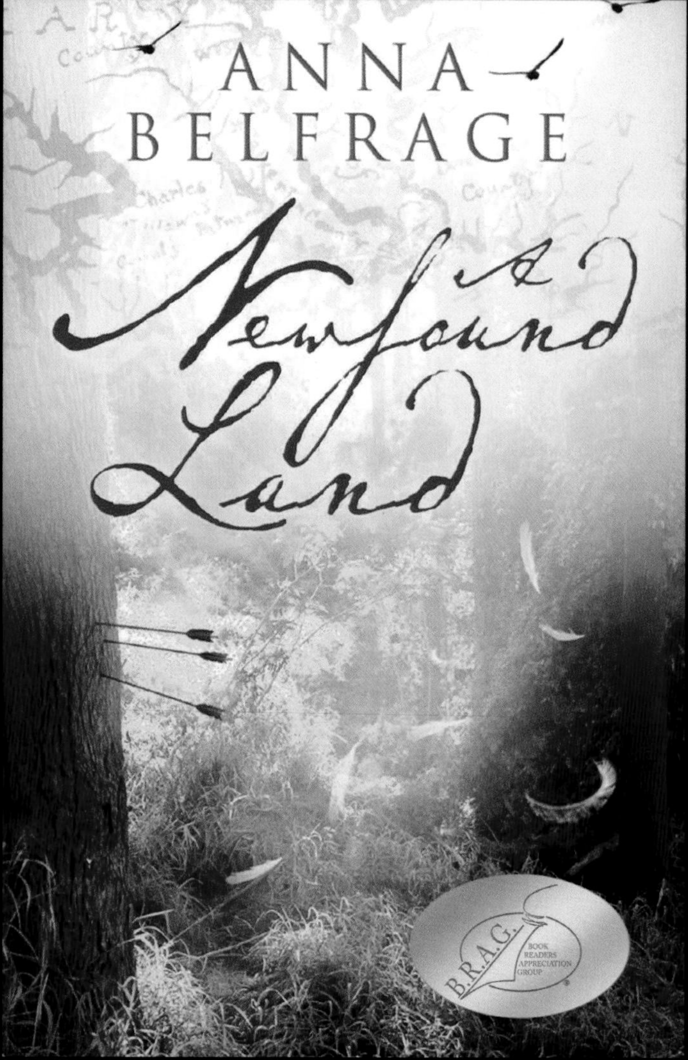

Colonizing a new land is not easy – even less so for reluctant time traveler Alex. But here she is, in Colonial Maryland where life is no walk in the park, not even with her beloved husband, Matthew Graham at her side. Things become increasingly complicated for both Alex and Matthew when people from their past make an unexpected entrance. And when the ruthless and evil Burley brothers set their sight on Matthew, this new life of theirs becomes way too dangerous.

www.annabelfrage.com

Swedish Christmas Saffron Buns

Yields 3 dozen

INGREDIENTS

3½ tsp yeast
⅔ cup of butter
2 cups milk
1 tsp saffron
½ tsp salt
¾ cup plus 1 tbsp of sugar
1 egg - whisked.
¼ cup raisins
4 to 4¼ cups all-purpose flour
1 egg with 1 tbsp water for egg wash

DIRECTIONS

1. Melt the butter, add the milk and heat carefully until it's "finger warm" or warm on your wrist.
2. Crumble or spoon the yeast into a bowl, add some of the milk/butter, dissolve the yeast before adding the rest of the liquid.
3. Mix sugar, salt and ground saffron. Mixing the saffron with the sugar prior to adding to the mix increases its aromatic properties.
4. Add sugar, salt, saffron to the liquid. Add a whisked egg. Add raisins and about half the flour. Mix thoroughly. Add the rest of the flour bit by bit, kneading the dough until it no longer sticks to the bowl but still is slightly sticky.
5. Powder some flour on top, set to rise under a towel for 45 minutes.
6. Divide up the dough in 36 pieces. Roll each piece into 6-8" in length and about the thickness of your thumb/index finger (depending on how thick your fingers are), which you then curl into an 8 (curl one end clockwise, the other anti-clockwise).
7. Place each bun on a parchment lined cookie sheet.
8. Decorate the centre of each curl with a raisin - like an "eye". Leave to rise another 20 minutes on the baking tin under a towel.
9. Wash with whisked egg and bake at 425F for 7-10 minutes until slightly golden.

Recipe Courtesy of Anna Belfrage

Annabeth is a hopeless romantic who believes in soul mates. She's been writing to hers since she was 16. Now 34, she's still holding out hope of finding Mr. Right despite her trust issues due to a past traumatic experience. When she meets Alex, she thinks her quest may finally be at an end. Soon she's working in close quarters with Alex and her long ago ex, Nick. Fighting attraction to one, loathing for the other, Annabeth is forced to face her old insecurities while keeping an eye on a scheming frienemy bent on derailing her hopes and dreams.

www.nicoleevelina.com

Been Searching For You

"It is a romantic party to meet and fall in love. Chicago's Drake Hotel with Dazzling spotlights and dancing heart shaped lights along with cocktails and tasty Hors D'oeuvres".

From *Been Searching For You*

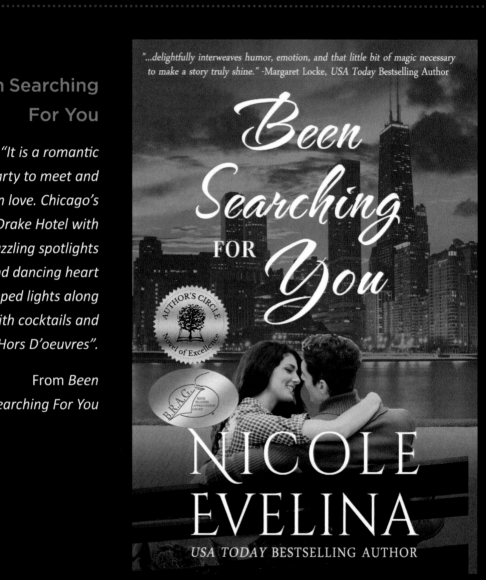

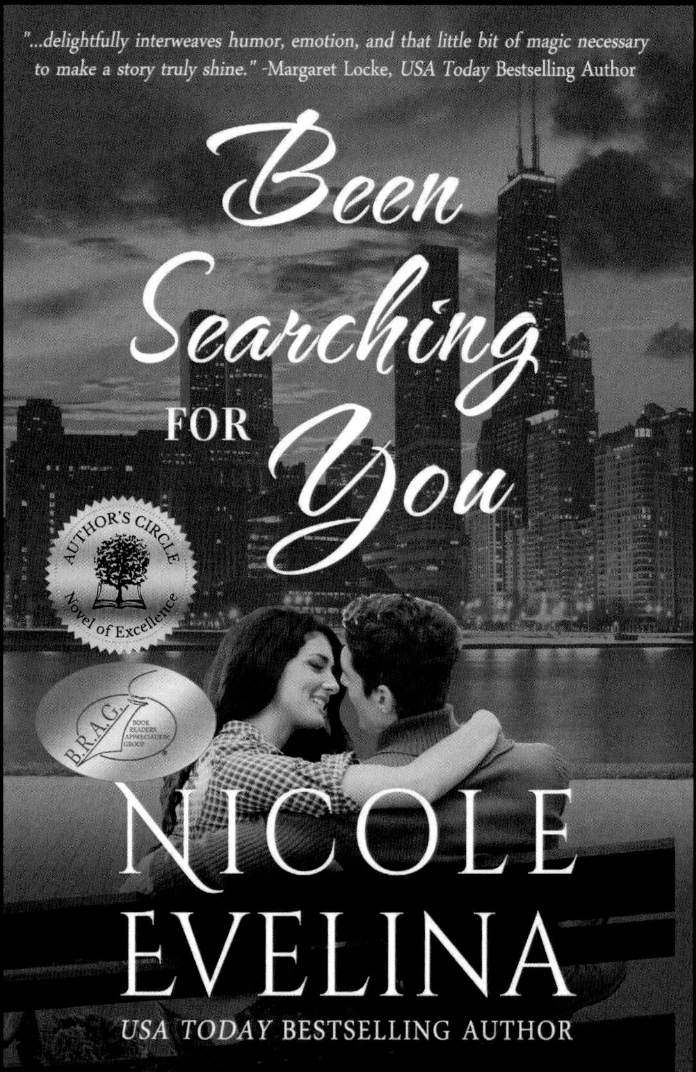
"...delightfully interweaves humor, emotion, and that little bit of magic necessary to make a story truly shine." -Margaret Locke, USA Today Bestselling Author
Been Searching for You
AUTHOR'S CIRCLE
Novel of Excellence
B.R.A.G.
BOOK READERS APPRECIATION GROUP
NICOLE EVELINA
USA TODAY BESTSELLING AUTHOR

Savory Stuffed Mushrooms

INGREDIENTS

1½ lb Bella mushrooms
2 tbsp olive oil
3-4 tbsp chives or onion, minced
12 oz canned or frozen crabmeat or imitation crab, such as Dyna crab
⅔ cup breadcrumbs, finely shredded
2-3 tbsp mayonnaise
¼ tsp dried thyme
¼ tsp paprika
1 tsp salt
½ tsp pepper

Expandthetable Suggestions:
Make it kosher with crab substitute

DIRECTIONS

1. Preheat oven to 400F.
2. Remove mushroom stems and clean stems by running them under water and then drying. Wipe mushrooms caps clean with a damp towel.
3. Chop mushroom stems. Heat 1 tablespoons of oil in a pan over medium heat. Add stems and chives or onions to pan and sauté.
4. Put sautéed stems and chives in a bowl and add crab, breadcrumbs, mayonnaise, salt and pepper. Gently fold ingredients together. Add more mayonnaise if ingredients do not stick together.
5. Place mushrooms on parchment lined pan. Place a teaspoon or so of mixture in each mushroom. Place in oven and bake for 25-30 minutes.
6. The stuffed mushrooms can be made ahead of time and refrigerated uncooked and then baked before serving. You may need to add 8-10 minutes to cooking time.

Davinia's Duke

She would seduce him with strawberry jam. And marmalade, for one could not discount the excellence of cook's marmalade, a divine concoction of Seville oranges, both tart and sweet and utterly gooey.

From *Davinia's Duke*

A too-perfect Duke, an imperfect lady...is it the perfect match or a perfect disaster?

The Dukes of Everley always marry at thirty--but the current Duke has left choosing a bride far too late. Arriving at a country house party, he expects to find one suitable young lady to be the next Duchess. He doesn't expect to find the woman who was the bane of his life for a season and who might be the only woman who can save him from becoming a far too proper Duke.

www.shannondonnelly.com

Yorkshire Cakes – perfect with marmalade and jam.

INGREDIENTS

4 oz butter
1 pint milk
1 package yeast
3-4 cups flour
2 eggs
½ cup raisins or other dried fruit, optional

DIRECTIONS

1. Melt 4 oz of butter. Add the milk and the yeast.
2. Add 5 cups flour and beat in eggs. Knead on clean surface, adding in as much flour as the dough will take. Knead until the dough is smooth and elastic.
3. Place dough in buttered or oil sprayed bowl and cover and let rise in warm place that is free of drafts until dough is doubled in size. Punch down and knead again for a few moments.
4. Tear off fist sized pieces and shape each one into a round form.
5. Lay each cake on a parchment lined baking sheet so that the cakes do not touch. Slash 3 times across the top with a sharp knife. Cover again and let rise for 1 hour until the cakes are doubled
6. Brush with egg wash before baking (beat 1 egg)
7. Bake at 350F for 15-18 minutes until brown and when tapped, the sound is hollow.
8. Serve with butter and home-made marmalade.

Note: the dough will freeze well. Bring cakes to room temperature. Wrap each in plastic wrap and then place several cakes in a freezer bag. Store in freezer up to 3 months.

Her wounds are hidden. His scars are hardened. Neither wants romance. Selfless Eva would be shunned if her shameful secret were revealed. Disfigured Baseel lets nobody close, preferring fear to pity. Eva's Jewish family is destroyed, and she finds herself sold into slavery. .Baseel is the majordomo of the merchant who acquires Eva and her brother. Eva's puzzled cat decides a lack of offspring is the cause of her mistress' misery and sets out to woo the dominant human lion with half-eaten prey. Surely Baseel will mate with Eva when he sees she belongs to a pride of good hunters?

www.emilylcotton.com

Eva's Secret

A tagine is a round-bellied clay pot whose lid features a long, narrow chimney. It is used by the peoples of North Africa (and historical Al-Andalus) to slow-cook over a banked fire.

Fortunately, you don't need a special vessel, nor a banked fire, to make a tagine today!

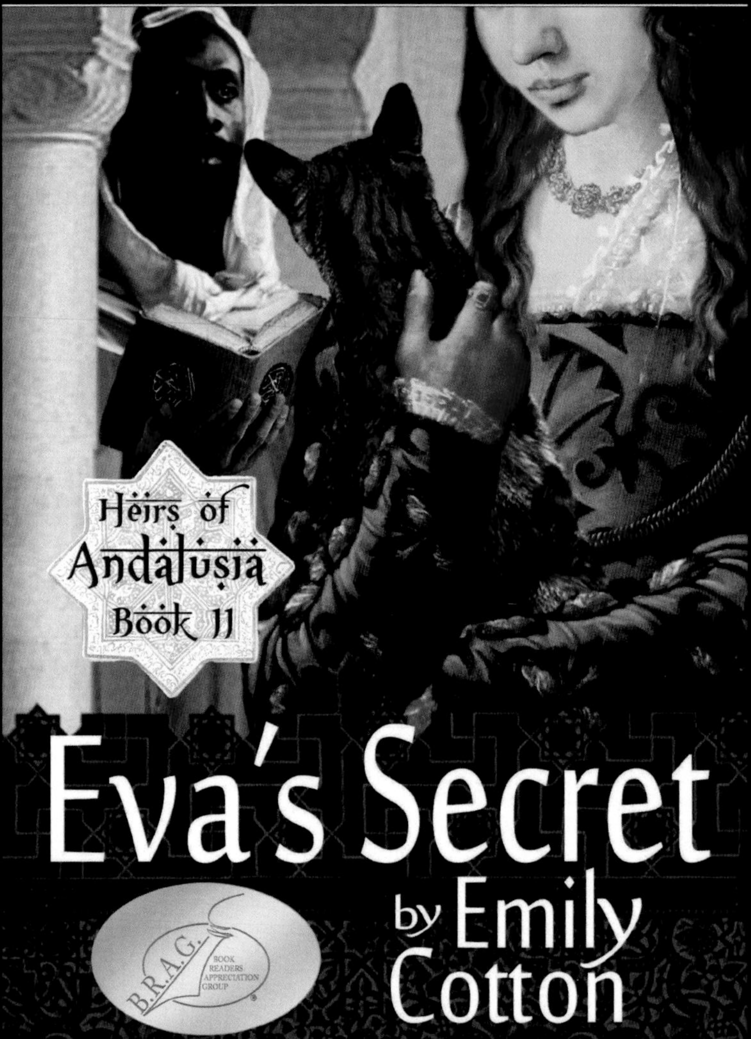

Moroccan Stew

INGREDIENTS

Ras-el-hanout spice mix

2 tsp ground cumin
2 tsp ground ginger
2 tsp salt
1 tsp black pepper
1 tsp cinnamon
1 tsp ground coriander seeds
1 tsp ground allspice
1 tsp cardamom
1 tsp turmeric
½ tsp ground cloves
½ tsp cayenne

Stew

1 medium eggplant, peeled and cubed
1 lb lamb, chicken or beef, cubed
1 tbsp olive oil
1 medium onion, chopped
1 leek, cleaned, dark green cut off (save for soup stock) and white and light green chopped
½ lb celery, chopped
3 garlic cloves, chopped
1 tbsp ras-el-hanout
½ lb carrots, chopped
¼ cup pine nuts, toasted
¼ cup raisins, dried figs, dates or apricots
1 tsp kosher salt
½ cup broth
1 cup couscous, very small size or Israeli couscous

DIRECTIONS

1. Place cubed eggplant in a colander in a sink or in a bowl. Salt the eggplant and let soak for 15 minutes. Rinse salt off eggplant.
2. Sear meat in a pot until browned on all sides. Remove to a plate and reserve.
3. Add olive oil and warm over medium heat. Add onion and leek and cook until soft. Add celery and garlic and continue to cook for 2-3 more minutes, adding more olive oil if needed. Add ras-el-hanout and salt and stir to coat vegetables. Remove from pot and reserve.
4. Add more olive oil to coat bottom of pan. Add eggplant and cook, stirring, until pieces are slightly browned.
5. Preheat oven to 350F. Place meat, vegetable mix and eggplant in the tagine or oven proof covered dish. Add carrots and raisins or other dried fruit.
6. Toast pine nuts for 3-4 minutes over medium heat in the previously used pot. Add to stew. Pour broth over the stew, cover and place in the oven for 3 hours or until meat is very tender. You may also place this stew in a crock pot and cook on low for 6 or more hours. Check occasionally to see if you need to add more liquid. Adjust seasoning.
7. Cook couscous according to package direction.
8. Place couscous in the center of a serving plate and the stew around it to serve.

Note: You may make your own ras-el-hanout or purchase the spice at your local supermarket.

Flux

Although Pam is not "overweight", she is definitely conscious of her body image and this low carb recipe is perfect for her- especially in the summer months!

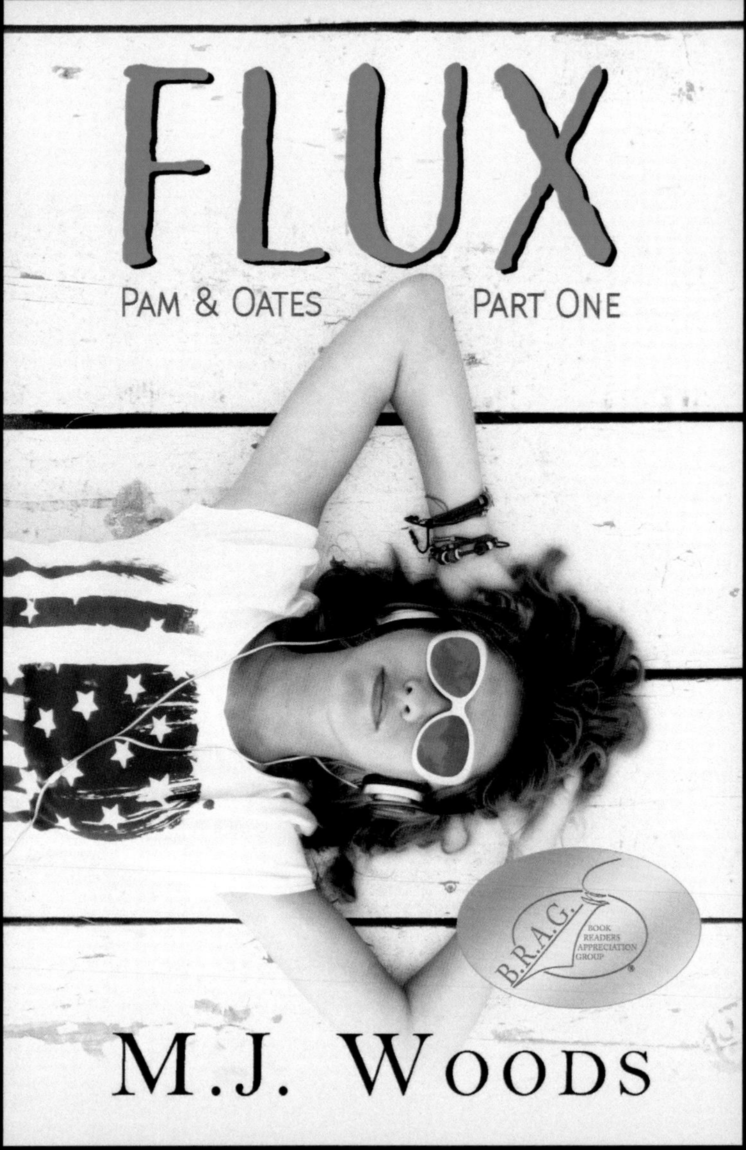

Three Days. Two Geeks. One Island.

A Contemporary New Adult Romance with humor and heat!

I'm Pam Clayton, a Canadian university student forever introduced as 'cute and smart', the girl with brown eyes and too-big thighs fated for a 'bright future'...until fate decides to shake things up. Gorgeous tech genius Daryl Oates drops into my orbit just as plans for my fourth year of study fall apart. My certain future becomes a question mark while Daryl proves the sexy brand of smart guy I fantasized about is real. Is it lasting love or just a temporary state of Flux?

www.mjwoodsbooks.com

Cauliflower and Potato Salad

Serves 8

INGREDIENTS

Soup

1 cup sugar
1 cup hot water
3 tsp kosher salt
½ cup white vinegar
1 tsp pepper

Seasoning

1 tsp celery salt
2 large cloves garlic, minced

Salad

¼ medium Vidalia onion, minced
1 cup mayonnaise
1 green or red bell peppers, finely sliced
1 carrot, finely sliced or grated
2 stalks celery, chopped
3 lbs potatoes, boiled, cooled and sliced. Peel if desired.
1 small head of cauliflower, cored and broken into florets

DIRECTIONS

1. Boil potatoes until a fork easily pierces the skin but before they will fall apart. Drain. Peel if desired. Cool.
2. Steam or roast cauliflower until soft but still holds its shape. Drain and cool.
3. Mix together sugar and hot water, stirring to dissolve.
4. Add salt, vinegar, pepper, celery salt, garlic, onions and mayonnaise. Mix together until lumpy.
5. Add peppers, carrots and celery. Mix together. Pour over sliced potatoes and cauliflower florets. Gently mix. Adjust salt and pepper to taste.
6. Let stand for 3 hours or overnight in refrigerator before serving.

Note: Potatoes absorb liquid. You may have to add a bit more *soup* if it looks dry.

Expandthetable Suggestions:

Lower the calories further by using olive oil mayonnaise

Make it even tastier by crumbling crisp bacon over the top.

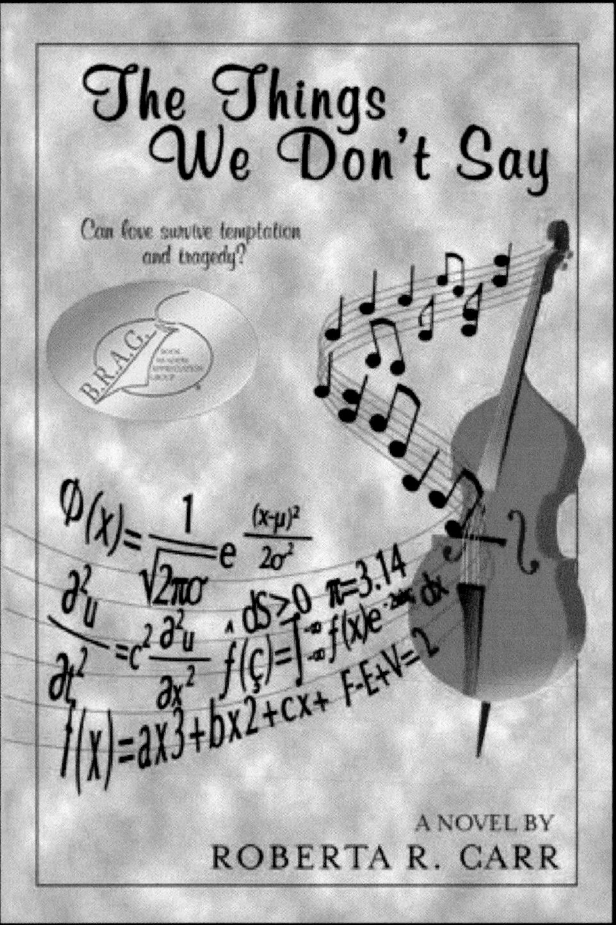

The Things We Don't Say

"Oh! I almost forgot." Lilia retrieved a large Ziploc bag from her backpack. "I have a surprise for you." Matt's mouth watered when he saw the contents. "Are those what I think they are?"

"Uh-huh. Your favorite. I baked 'em last night."

From *The Things We Don't Say*

Photo Courtesy of
Roberta R. Carr

Ranger Cookies

Yields 4 dozen cookies

INGREDIENTS

1 cup of unsalted butter
1 cup brown sugar
1 cup white sugar
2 eggs
1 tsp vanilla
2 cups flour
1 tsp baking soda
1 tsp baking powder
½ tsp salt
2 cups uncooked oats
1 cup of Rice Krispies
2 cups shredded cocoanut
1 cup of chocolate chips

DIRECTIONS

1. Preheat oven to 375F degrees
2. Mix thoroughly the first 9 ingredients and then add the remaining 4 ingredients.
3. Drop by spoon on greased cookie sheet and bake at 375F for 8-11 minutes, or until golden brown.
4. Cool on baking sheets for 2 minutes before moving them to wire racks to cool completely. Enjoy!

Courtesy of Roberta R. Carr

SCIENCE FICTION

GENRE

Broken Portal in Rocky Mountain Park
    Trout Almandine

Lady of Devices
    California Christmas Cake

Mythicals
    Creamy Mushroom Soup

Paradise Girl
    Pork Chops and Apples

Smoke in Her Eyes
    Hint of Summertime Linguini

Spindown
    Cajun Jambalaya

The Time Travel Trailer
    Applesauce Cake

Broken Portal In Rocky Mountain Park

Before venturing into a stone portal which will take Sophie Anderson 140 years into the past, she and her friend eat at her favorite restaurant The Brown Palace where they both order Trout Almandine. It is a pretty simple recipe that is perfect for the Rocky Mountain west!

1877–a smear of blood. Mutating bacteria. 2017–unrelenting plague. The last pandemic.

The world's worst nightmare, a disease without a cure–a mutated version of Rocky Mountain spotted fever with an 80% death rate. Can a time traveler change history by destroying the disease at its inception? It's a gamble, but worth a try. Venturing into a stone portal, Sophie Anderson travels through time arriving 140 years in the past. She meets Colorado characters: Isabella Bird, a writer and adventurer; One-Eyed Rocky Mountain Jim, a trapper; the Earl of Dunraven, a wealthy Anglo-Irishman; Albert Bierstadt, a famous American artist.

Some will help, others will try to kill her.

www.pamelabeglinski.com

Trout Almandine

Serves 4

INGREDIENTS

½ cups sliced almonds
½ cup flour
½ tsp salt
¼ tsp pepper
4 trout fillets
2 tbsp butter
1 lemon

DIRECTIONS

1. Toast almonds in skillet until lightly browned. Set aside.
2. Mix flour, salt and pepper. Dredge both sides of trout fillets in flour mixture.
3. Melt butter in the skillet. Add trout fillets and brown on each side. Place trout fillets on a platter, scattering almonds on top of each fillet.
4. Serve with a green salad or asparagus baked in butter.

Dairy free: Use non-dairy margarine or vegetable oil in place of butter.

Lady of Devices

The humble fruitcake is universally reviled in the US, but in England and Canada, it's a beloved centuries-old tradition. This delicious blond fruitcake is one the characters enjoy and is based on the author's family recipe.

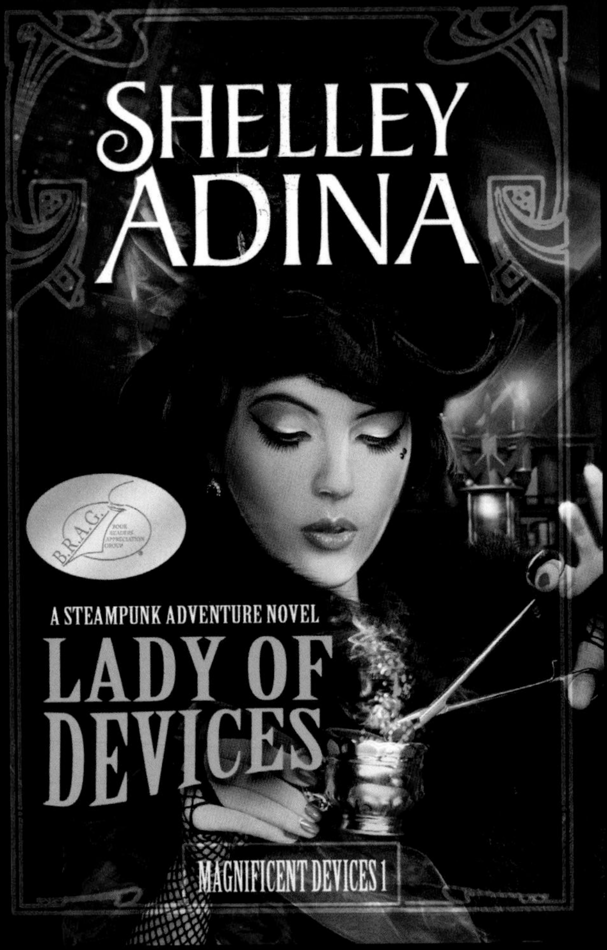

It's 1889, and Lady Claire Trevelyan's talents, sadly, lie not in the ballroom, but in the laboratory, where her experiments have a habit of blowing up. When her father gambles the estate on the combustion engine though everyone knows the world runs on steam, Claire finds herself out in the streets with nothing to her name but her steam landau and her second-best hat. When she barters her skills for a street gang's protection, it's not long before a new leader rises in the London underworld, known as the Lady of Devices ... a double life Claire must keep secret if she is to become the assistant to a world-renowned scientist.

www.shelleyadina.com

California Christmas Cake

The night before:

3 cups each dark and golden raisins
1 cup brandy, bourbon, whiskey, sherry, or clear fruit juice
Toss raisins in alcohol or juice over low heat, remove from stove and soak overnight.
1 cup coarsely shredded unsweetened coconut
1 cup milk

Soak coconut in milk overnight in small bowl in fridge.

In the morning:

Fruit:

2 cups chopped dried fruit (peaches, apricots, apples, pears, or your favorites)
1 8-oz tub glace red cherries
1 8-oz tub citron peel
1 cup chopped pecans
2 cups *sifted* all-purpose flour

Mix all the fruit in a very large bowl and toss with sifted flour.

Batter:

3 cups butter, softened
4½ cups granulated sugar
9 eggs
3 tsp each vanilla and almond extract
Cream butter and sugar. Add eggs 3 at a time, beating well after each. Add vanilla and almond flavorings.

6 cups *sifted* all-purpose flour
6 tsp baking powder
1 ½ tsp salt

Re-sift the flour with baking powder and salt.

DIRECTIONS

1. Add flour mixture to the creamed mixture, alternating with the coconut and milk mixture. Combine batter thoroughly into fruit. It will be heavy; you may need to use both hands instead of a spoon.
2. Preheat oven to 275F and place a pie pan half filled with water on the lowest shelf to make a moist environment. Line 6 loaf pans with a layer of brown paper, then a layer of waxed paper. You could also use a single layer of parchment paper. Fill pans with fruit batter and bake for 90 minutes. Test for doneness. If toothpick does not come out clean, continue to bake.
3. When baked, remove from oven and cool in pans. When cool, baste each cake with 2 tablespoons of whiskey or other liquid. Remove from pans with paper and wrap in zip bags or airtight container. Once a week, baste each cake with 2 tablespoons more liquid. Store for one month or more before eating. Keeps up to 4 months in airtight container. Slice and serve.

Recipe Courtesy of Shelley Adina

Journalist Jack March makes a stunning discovery: that all the creatures of myth and legend are real! Fairies, pixies, trolls, werewolves, ogres, and vampires are alien exiles—serving out banishment disguised in flesh-suits enabling them to live among the planet's natives. Jack also makes a horrendous discovery: they have decided that the native "terminal species" must be eradicated before it ruins its planet's ecology. In this riveting sci-fi/fairy tale, Jack joins with sympathetic fairies, pixies, and ogres to attempt to save the planet from the "mythicals," as well as the mysterious alien cabal known as the Pilgrims.

www.dennismeredith.com

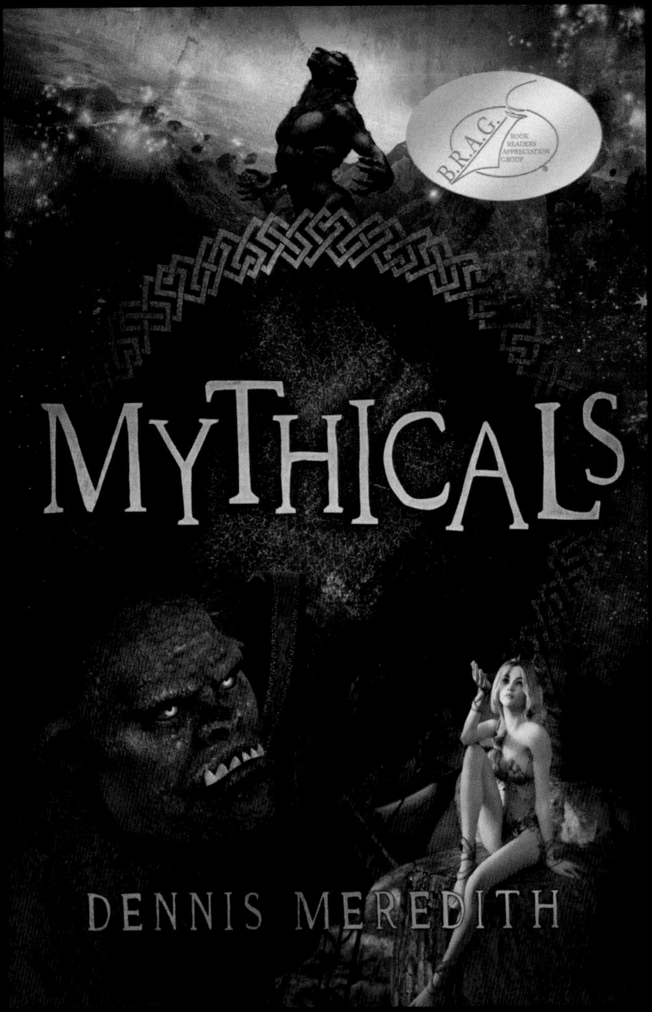

Mythicals

Rings of mushrooms growing are called Fairy Rings. These were thought to be little realms of fairies and elves. They danced and frolicked within the rings. They randomly appear and have been a part of mythical folklore for centuries.

Creamy Mushroom Soup

Serves 5-6

INGREDIENTS

2 oz dried porcini mushrooms with water to cover
3 tbsp olive oil
2 cloves garlic, minced
1 small onion, finely chopped
1 stalk celery, chopped
8 oz button mushrooms, cleaned and chopped
2 tbsp flour
3 cups vegetable stock
1 tsp kosher salt
½ tsp dried thyme or leaves from 3 fresh sprigs
¼ tsp freshly ground pepper
Pinch of cayenne pepper
Fresh thyme and parsley for garnish

DIRECTIONS

1. Soak porcini mushrooms in warm water for 1 hour. Make sure that mushrooms are totally covered with water. Drain and reserve liquid. Trim woody stems from mushrooms and chop remaining mushroom tops. Strain liquid with cheese cloth or a very fine sieve.
2. Warm 2 tablespoons of olive oil in a soup pot. Add garlic and onion, cook for 1 minute until they begin to soften. Add mushrooms and cook for about 3 minutes, until the mushrooms start to brown. Remove to a bowl.
3. Add 1 tablespoon of oil to soup pot. Melt and sprinkle flour on oil and whisk quickly to a paste. Reduce heat to medium. Add the stock a little at a time, whisking out the lumps and stirring until smooth. Add porcini mushroom liquid to pot and stir to combine.
4. Simmer stock for 2-3 minutes. Add mushrooms back to the soup pot and cook for 2-3 minutes until stock thickens to become creamy. Cook stirring until the soup is completely heated but does not boil. Taste and adjust seasoning. Cool. Leave chunk as is or purée with immerser in pot or with blender to a velvety smoothness.
5. Garnish with fresh thyme and parsley. Serve with homemade croutons if desired.

This soup is vegan.

A fatal virus ravages Kerryl's community, wiping out friends and family. Left on her own, she starts to lose her grip on reality. She's convinced that she, too, will soon fall prey to the infection, and decides to record in a diary what she thinks will be her last days. She imagines a reader and calls him Adam. As the empty days pass, Adam becomes increasingly real to her until his presence dominates her life. She is elated when she receives what she thinks is an invitation for a date and sets out across the moor to meet Adam, and her fate. 'The truth is blurred in this captivating psychological thriller, which saves its final surprise until a twist at the very end.'

www.phillfeatherstone.net

Paradise Girl

The Paradise Girl is a tragic apocalyptic tale. Kerryl and her brother lived on a farm with chickens and cows and plenty of vegetables in the garden. Before the virus arrived they had plenty of wonderful healthy meals. Perhaps even something like...

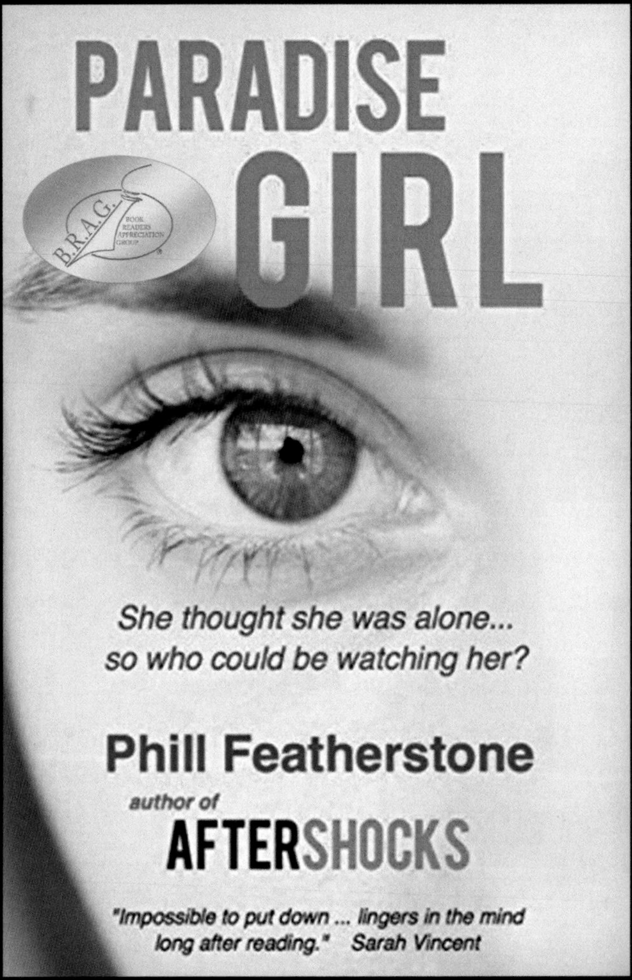

Apples and Honey Pork Chops

Serves 6

INGREDIENTS

6 bone in pork chops – thick, ¾ inches
2 tbsp olive oil
2 tbsp butter
Salt and pepper
1 large Red onion, sliced
1 tsp sage
1 tsp thyme
½ tsp rosemary
3-4 Gala apples, unpeeled, cored and sliced
1 cup of white wine, apple cider or broth
2 tbsp honey

Expandthetable Suggestions:
For Apples and Honey Chicken: Use 8-10 chicken thighs in place of pork

DIRECTIONS

1. Add oil to cast iron or heavy skillet.
2. Generously salt and pepper chops and place in skillet.
3. Do not crowd pan or chops won't brown properly. If pan is not big enough, do in batches
4. Cook for about 5 minutes on each side.
5. Remove chops, melt oil and add onions, sage, thyme and rosemary. Cook until onions begin to brown. Add apples and cooked until softened.
6. Remove apples and onions mixture and add pork chops. Add apple and onion mixture on top.
7. Add liquid and honey and cook for about 15 minutes turning once.
8. Remove from skillet. Turn heat to high and cook, reducing the liquid and thickening it.
9. Serve with a spoonful of the reduced liquid, onions and apples mixture on top of each pork chop.

Smoke in Her Eyes

Nigel was still ranting about the government in between shoveling pasta into himself as if he hadn't seen food in a month. How someone so thin could eat so much was a mystery...

From *Smoke in Her Eyes*

Two men. One woman. A vicious cycle of love, hate, death, rebirth. Not a Happily Ever After in sight... Six months ago, Helle Madsen would have described herself as normal. Now she no longer knows if that terms applies, not after her entire life has been turned upside down by the reappearance of not one, but two, men from her very, very distant past.

www.annabelfrage.com

Hint of Summertime Linguini

Serves 5-6

INGREDIENTS

1 cup various vegetables chopped into bite sized pieces: broccoli, asparagus, cauliflower, zucchini, etc.
1 tbsp butter or oil
½ cup sliced almonds
¼ lb mushroom caps, cleaned
10 cherry tomatoes, halved
1-2 garlic cloves, crushed or minced
1 tbsp butter or olive oil
1 tsp salt
½ tsp pepper
¾ lb linguini
¾ cup cream
1 tsp chopped basil or ½ tsp dried
¼-⅓cup pasta water
⅓ cup grated Parmesan

DIRECTIONS

1. Steam vegetables al dente.
2. Melt butter. Add sliced almonds and toast over medium heat. Remove from heat.
3. In same pan, sauté mushrooms caps and remove from pan. Sauté cherry tomatoes adding oil as needed. After 2 minutes, add garlic, salt and pepper. Remove from heat when garlic is golden and tomatoes softened. Remove from pan.
4. Cook linguini according to package directions. Save water.
5. In mushroom-tomato pot, melt ¼ cup butter. Add back in tomatoes and garlic Add cream and basil. Stir. Add spaghetti to heated sauce, toss to cook. Add all veggies, toss gently until all is hot. Add pasta water as needed. Add Parmesan cheese.
6. Serve with extra cream or cheese.

Note: Can prepare everything ahead of time up to the sauce stage.

Expandthetable Suggestions:

Frutti di Mare: Add 8 shrimp, shelled and deveined, 12 littleneck clams, cleaned and/or 1 lb small mussels, cleaned

Add some wine: Add ½ cup dry white wine with tomatoes and garlic.

Spindown

The culture onboard the spaceship is truly a fusion of Spanish, French, and West African. Creole Jambalaya is a Fusion of these cultures and a tradition in Louisiana.

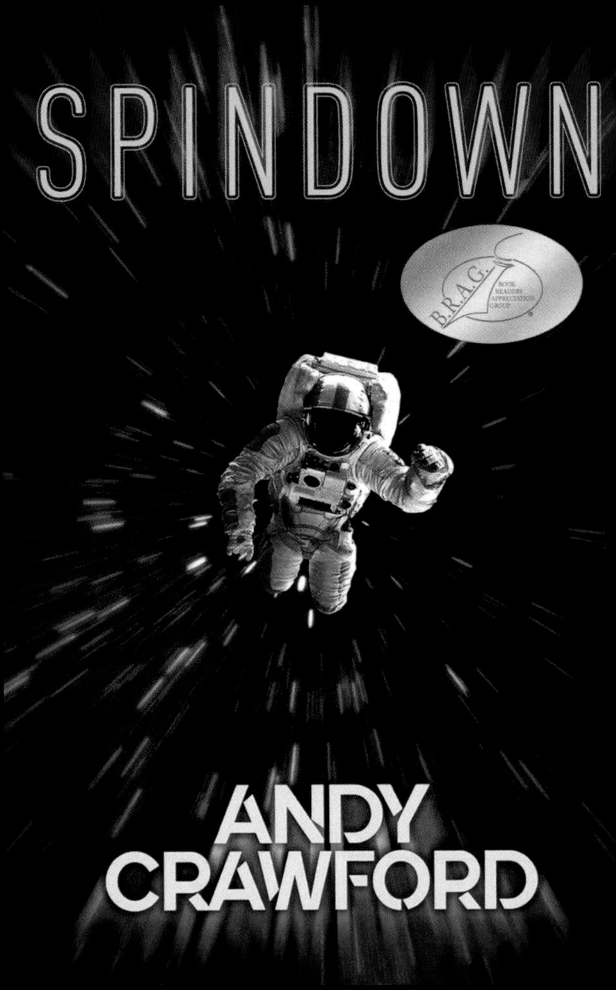

"Cyrus Konami is the Chief Inspector on the first colony vessel, Aotea, to leave Earth's solar system. Deep within the machinery of the ship, a suspicious death upends the routine on board. Mysterious signals from deep space add to the confusion, along with a series of debilitating malfunctions. Cy and Lieutenant Beatriz Mattoso dig into the deceased crewman's background, finding conflicting evidence. With an increasingly uncooperative populace, a shocking assassination attempt, and a spaceship falling apart around them, Cy and Bea must unravel secrets that threaten the lives of thousands before it's too late!"

www.amzn.to/32mxzSw

Creole Jambalaya

INGREDIENTS

1 tbsp extra-virgin olive oil
1 onion, chopped
2 bell (1 Red & 1 Green) peppers, chopped
½ cup diced celery
3 cloves minced garlic
1 lb boneless skinless chicken breasts, cut into 1" pieces
6 oz andouille sausage, sliced
2 tbsp tomato paste
2 cups low-sodium chicken stock
1 (15-oz) can crushed tomatoes
1 cup long grain rice
1 lb medium shrimp, peeled and deveined
2 green onions, thinly sliced

CREOLE SEASONING INGREDIENTS

½ tsp salt
½ tsp paprika
¼ tsp ground black pepper
½ tsp onion powder
¼ tsp cayenne pepper
½ tsp chili powder
1 tbsp dried oregano
¼ tsp dried thyme

DIRECTIONS

1. In a large pot over medium heat, heat oil. Add onion and bell peppers and season with salt and pepper. Cook until soft, about 5 minutes, then stir in chicken and season with salt, pepper, and oregano. Cook until the chicken is golden, about 5 minutes, then stir in andouille sausage, garlic, and tomato paste and cook until fragrant, about 1 minute more.
2. Add chicken broth, crushed tomatoes, rice. Reduce heat to medium low, cover with a tight-fitting lid, and cook until the rice is tender, and the liquid is almost absorbed, about 20 minutes.
3. Add the shrimp and cook until pink, 3 to 5 minutes.
4. Stir in green onions just before serving.
5. Creole food is not traditionally as spicy as Cajun but you can add more heat by adding more pepper or serving hot sauce separately so your guests may add as they like

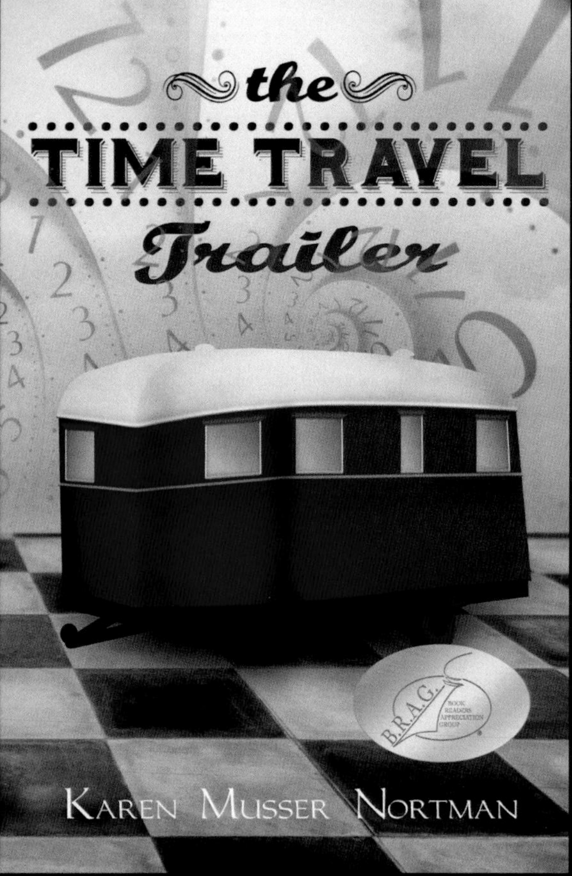

Time Travel Trailer

The Time Travel Trailer travels through the 30's, 40's, 50's and 60's! A stop at the county fair in the 1930's brings on memories of wonderful homecooked food, especially delicious Applesauce Cake.

Lynne McBriar buys a vintage camper in an effort to bond with her 14-year-old daughter, Dinah, in the wake of a separation from her husband. But to their shock, the trailer takes them back to the 1960s

Applesauce Cake

Yield 1 cake

INGREDIENTS

2 cups flour
½ cup raisins
1 tsp baking soda
2 tsp baking powder
½ tsp kosher salt
1 tsp cinnamon
½ tsp ginger
½ tsp ground cloves
1 cup brown sugar
1 cup unsweetened smooth or chunky applesauce
¾ cup vegetable oil
2 large eggs, at room temperature
1 tsp vanilla extract

DIRECTIONS

1. Preheat oven to 350F. Spray a 9" round pan with oil spray. Sprinkle with sugar on the bottom of the pan.
2. Soak raisins in warm water or a sweet liqueur, such as amaretto, with enough liquid to cover.
3. In a large bowl, mix together flour, baking soda, baking powder, salt, cinnamon, ginger and cloves.
4. In a separate bowl, mix together sugar, applesauce, oil, eggs and vanilla extract.
5. Fold the sugar mixture into the flour mixture.
6. Add the raisins; stir until just mixed.
7. Pour the batter into prepared pan and smooth top of batter with spatula. Bake for 35-40 minutes, until a toothpick inserted into the center comes out clean. Sprinkle confectioner's sugar on top, if desired.

THRILLER GENRE

A Black Bear Killer in Castaway County
    Mom's Fruit and Cream Pie

Blood Allegiance
    Arroz con Leche—Spanish Rice Pudding

The Covenant Within
    Clapshot

The Goliath Code
    German Spaetzle

The Second Wife
    Creamy Cardamom Chai

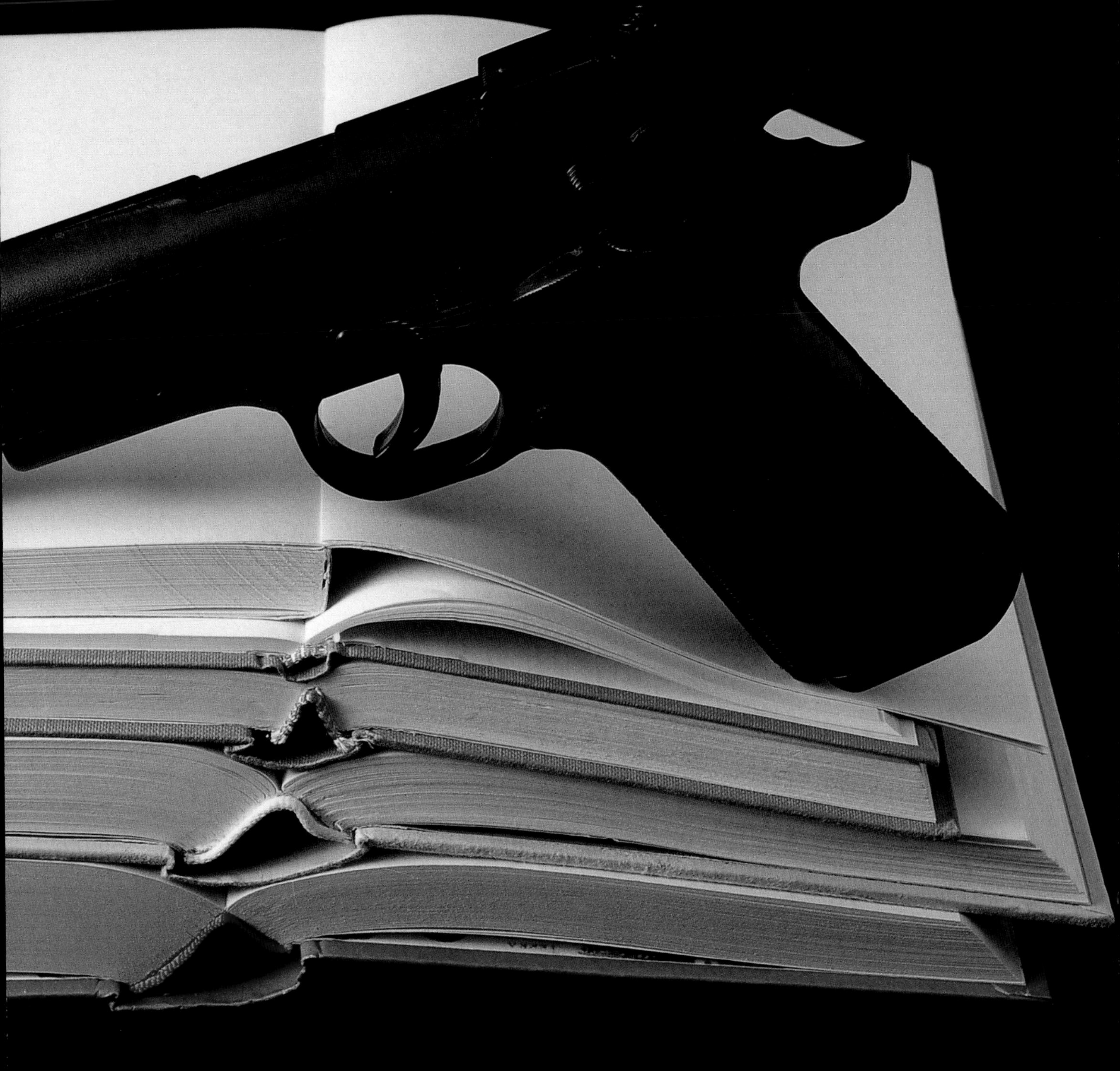

A Black Bear Killer in Castaway County

Cream pie is a staple of Truck Stop Food and Blueberries are Maine's official state fruit. Could there be a better combination for dessert?

Wendell "Dell" Hinton, sheriff of Castaway County, Maine, is sleeping when his phone rings in the middle of the night, alerting him to a multiple homicide at a local truck stop. As Dell, who has already solved a ten-year-old cold case during his first term, crawls out of bed, kisses his news anchor girlfriend goodbye, and leaves for the truck stop, he suspects a short night is about to turn into a very long day. When he arrives on the gruesome scene, the sheriff begins following a trail of clues that soon leads him to believe he may be dealing with a professional killer rather than an amateur thief.

Mom's Fruit & Cream Pie

Photo Courtesy of indieBRAG

INGREDIENTS

4 cups fresh Blueberries (or peaches, pears or bananas)
1 packet Knox gelatin mix
½ cup sugar
1 pint heavy cream
1 pie crust, homemade or store bought

DIRECTIONS

1. Pre-heat oven to 425F.
2. Place fruit to nearly fill pie shell. Leave space around/between fruit pieces to allow filling to seep in. (Just don't pack fruit tightly.) Fill to near the top of the pie shell.
3. In a measuring cup, mix sugar and 1 packet of Knox gelatin mix. (The amount of sugar will be ¼ cup to ⅔ cup depending upon the sweetness of the fruit you use. Don't over sweeten, as some fruits are extremely sweet in season.)
4. Sprinkle sugar mix over the fruit, filling in the spaces as you go.
5. Then pour about a pint of heavy whipping cream over the fruit. Be sure you fill in the spaces and wash the sugar mix down into fruit.
6. Bake at 425F until the top starts to brown and you can see a few bubbles in the center of pie. Baking time should be around 30-40 minutes.
7. Remove and let cool a good while. Refrigerate after the pie cools to ensure it gels up well. It's best served cold from refrigerator.
8. To be extra decadent. Serve whipped cream on top!

Recipe Courtesy of John Hickman

When the lead Santa Clara criminalist is found dismembered at a local Mexican restaurant and the crime scene is tagged with gang graffiti, Detective Darcy Lynch knows he's way out of his depth. But what looked like an isolated homicide becomes a blood bath when another member of the unit is gunned down and a drone crashes into a SJPD helicopter. If Lynch fails to hunt down the killer, not only his entire career could be at stake, but one of the most vicious California gangs may execute his entire team.

www.elinbarnes.com

Blood Allegiance

One of the most popular sweet desserts in the Mexican culture is Mexican Rice Pudding which would certainly have been served in the Santa Clara restaurant – scene of the murder!

Arroz con Leche—Spanish Rice Pudding

Serves 8.

INGREDIENTS

12 cups milk
1 cinnamon stick
Peel of ½ lemon
Pinch of salt
⅔ cup short grain rice
1¼ cup sugar
2 tbsp Grand Marnier
1 tsp vanilla extract
½ cup golden raisins
2 tbsp butter

DIRECTIONS

1. In a heavy pot, bring milk to a boil with cinnamon sticks, lemon peel and salt. Lower heat to a simmer.
2. Add rice and simmer very slowly, uncovered. Stir frequently with a wooden spoon to prevent sticking.
3. Cook for 3 hours. Stir every 10 minutes.
4. Add sugar, Grand Marnier, vanilla extract and raisins. Heat 10 minutes more. Pudding should be the consistency of soft custard.
5. Add butter and stir until melted. Cool to room temperature, stirring.
6. Sprinkle each serving with cinnamon and sugar.

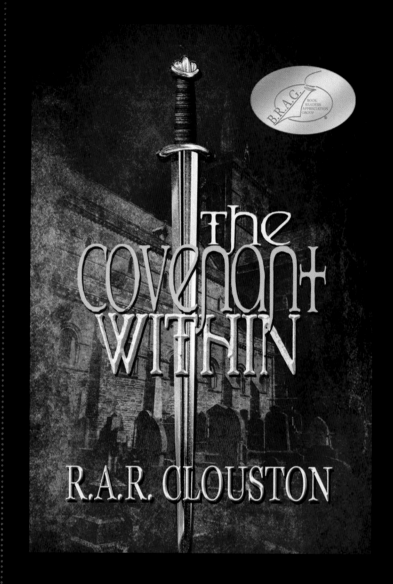

Clapshot

INGREDIENTS

1 small turnip, roughly 18 oz (i.e. the size of a grapefruit)
3 medium potatoes, roughly 1 lb (Desiree are of course the best for mashing, but mealy potatoes, such as Golden Wonder or Records, are what were traditionally grown in Scotland)
1 medium brown onion (optional)
Small bunch of chives (optional)
Butter
Salt and pepper
Nutmeg (optional)

DIRECTIONS

1. Prepare the turnip by removing the outer skin, then cut it into small and even cubes.
2. Peel the potatoes and chop them into cubes. Boil both vegetables in salted water in separate pots.
3. Meanwhile peel and slice the onion as thin as you can, then fry it slowly in a pan with a little butter, or cooking oil, until well browned, sweet and crispy.
4. When the turnip and potato are soft, when they can be pierced easily with a sharp knife, drain them and leave them to steam for 5 minutes to help get rid of any excess water.
5. Mash the turnip and potato together in a pot over a low heat, this helps to remove any excess water, and to keep it hot. Add a generous knob of butter, a grating of nutmeg and grinding of black pepper.
6. Stir half the onions through and save the rest for the top. Check for seasoning and serve sprinkled with the remaining onions and chives.

THE WORLD ENDED THREE DAYS AFTER HER 16TH BIRTHDAY

In the aftermath of a devastating natural disaster, one girl fights to survive in an isolated mountain town where thousands are dead and hundreds are missing. As society descends into the chaos of a post-apocalyptic nightmare, neighbor soon turns against neighbor in a frantic grab for precious resources. But Sera Donner will risk everything to protect the people she loves, even if that means sacrificing herself to the greatest evil mankind has ever known.

Prepare yourself for the horrors of The Goliath Code.

www.amzn.to/2TeNsGu

The Goliath Code

" Hilda brought out bowls of something called spatzle. I must have been German in another life because it was the best macaroni and cheese I'd ever tasted."

From *The Goliath Code*

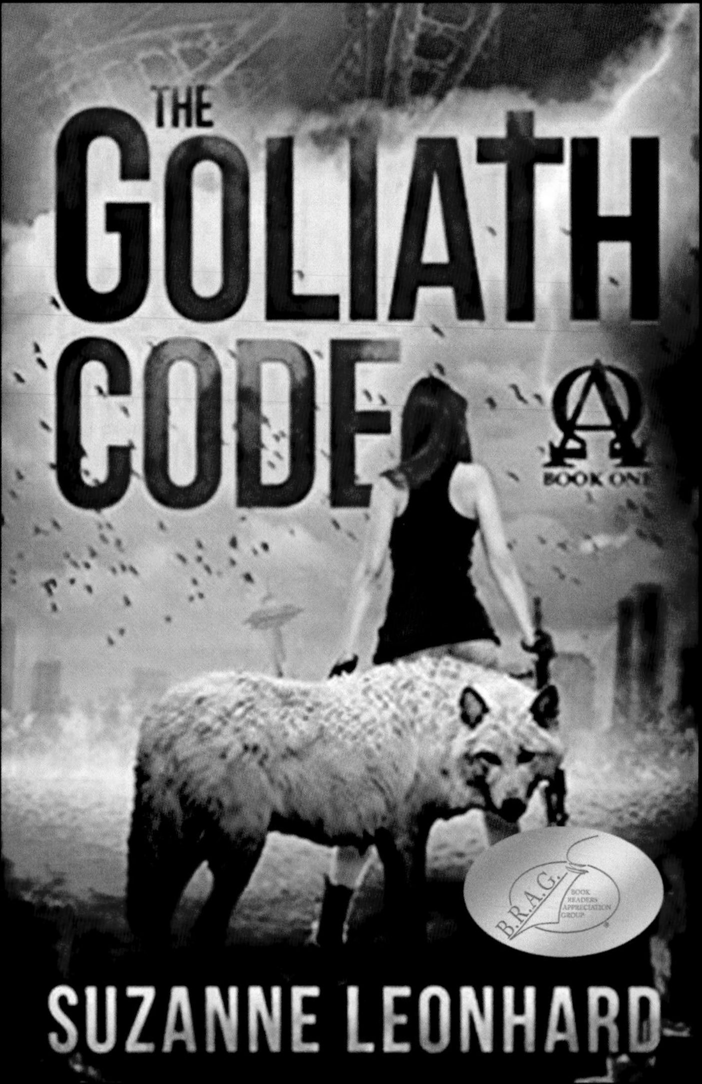

German Spaetzle

INGREDIENTS

5 lightly beaten eggs
½ cup of milk
2 cups of all-purpose flour
2 tsp salt
⅛ tsp of pepper
8 cups of liquid (water or be creative using chicken broth, carrot juice, beet juice, which all add a nice flavor)
Parsley or nutmeg, optional garnish

DIRECTIONS

1. Lightly beat the eggs and milk together.
2. Incorporate the flour, salt and pepper.
3. Bring the 8 cups of liquid to a gentle boil.
4. Pour the mixture into a colander and push through the holes with a wooden spoon. You can purchase a Spaetzle maker if you like but it is not necessary.
5. The Spaetzle is done when it floats to the top of the pot.
6. Remove with a slotted spoon.
7. Mix with butter and parsley and serve.

Spaetzle is delicious mixed with cheese, bacon bits, cooked onions or serve with chicken or beef gravy.

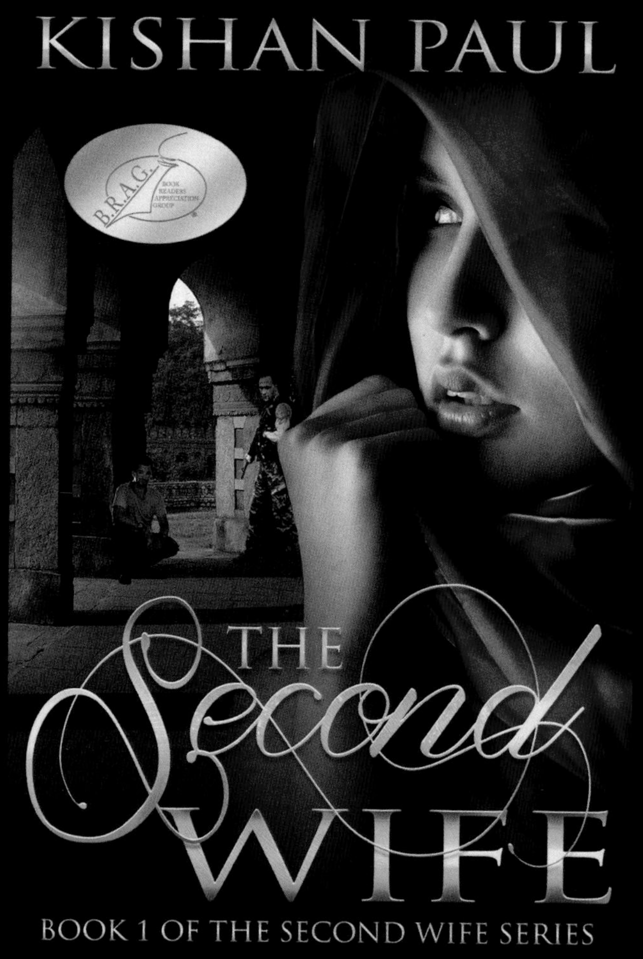

The Second Wife

Drinking Chai every morning is not just a habit but an obsession! This creamy brew is often found in homes in Pakistan, India, and several countries in the Middle East. The Second Wife Series would not be complete without Chai.

Abducted by her client...

Psychologist Alisha Dimarchi fights not only to survive but to protect the people she now considers family. She endures her traumatic existence by retreating to memories of the only man she has ever loved—a man she believes no longer loves her.

After two years of searching...

David is forced to consider a life without his wife until an unexpected visitor gives him the hope he's ached for. With the aid of a mercenary, he crosses oceans in search of the woman he loves.

Lives will be lost and hearts broken in this chilling suspenseful thrill ride.

This book contains graphic scenes and very sensitive subject matters.

www.kishanpaul.net

Creamy Cardamom Chai

INGREDIENTS

1 cup of milk
2 cardamom pods (more or less according to your preference)
½ tsp of Assam loose-leaf tea (more or less according to your preference of strength)
sugar as needed

DIRECTIONS

1. Put 1 cup of milk in saucepan (if using low fat milk, keep heat on low to avoid burning). Remove the shells from the cardamom pods and discard the shells.
2. Crush the seeds and put it in a saucepan with milk.
3. Heat the milk and add tea leaves and sugar once milk has warmed and stir.
4. Once the mixture rises shut off the heat, strain the leaves, and enjoy the tea.

INDEX

APPETIZERS /HORS D'OEUVRES

Bean dip, Baked Coulommiers – The Pretender, 115
Savory Stuffed Mushrooms-Been Searching For You, 155
Spinach Cheese Pockets –Shadow Weaver, 29
Wonton Cups Hors D'oeuvres- Tale Half Told, 79

BREAD

Banana Bread – Oh Susannah: It's in the bag, 5
Christmas Saffron Buns – A Newfound Land, 153
Corn Bread – Blind Tribute, 45
French Bread - Line by Line, 55
Hearty Biscuits – Dirt, 49
Orange Glazed Sweet Rolls – Hush Girl: It's Only A Dream, 127
Scottish Oat Scones – A Mistake of Consequences, 41

DESSERT

Applesauce Cake- The Time Travel Trailer, 179
Arroz con Leche—Spanish Rice Pudding -Blood Allegiance, 185
Boston Cream Pie – Tupelo Honey, 97
California Christmas Cake – Lady of Devices, 169
Chocolate Vampire Cupcakes –The Outcasts, 31
Christmas Stollen – Immigrant Soldier, 51
Dutch Apple Tart – The Lover's Portrait, 131
Fairy Muffins – Piccadilly and the Jolly Raindrops, 7
Lavender Sweet Tea Cakes – Circle of Nine – Beltany, 25
Molasses Cookies – In the Company of Like-Minded Women, 93
Mom's Fruit and Cream Pie- A Black Bear Killer in Castaway County, 183
New York Cheesecake – Death by Times New Roman, 125
Pirates Rum Cake – Sea Witch, 61
Ranger Cookies –The Things We Don't Say, 163
Traditional English Trifle – That Scoundrel Émile Dubois, 83
Yorkshire Cakes - Davinia's Duke, 157

DOG TREAT

Peanut Butter Treats – Unleashed, 99

DRINK

Bloody Mary- Bloody Mary, 73
Creamy Cardamom Chai- The Second Wife, 191
Dark and Stormy Cocktail – The Muse, 81
Tropical Fruit Smoothie – Andee the Aquanaut, 103

FISH

Gravlax – Jøssing Affair, 63
Mediterranean Sea Bass- Imperial Passions, 53
Newfoundland Fish Cakes – None of Us the Same, 57

MAIN COURSE

A Simplified Haggis, Tatties 'n Neeps - Scotland's Guardians, 27
Beanie Burgers- Feasible Planet, 139
Bubble and Squeak - Peggy Pinch, The Policeman's Wife, 129
Creole Jambalaya – Spindown, 177
Cannelloni -Rebels Against Tyranny, 59
Charlies Mama's Grits – Bulwark, 23
Chicken Pesto with Pine Nuts- Good-bye Pittsburgh, 89
Chicken Stir Fry – Like to Die, 77
Colonial Southern Stew – Little Miss History Travels to Mount Vernon, 109
Diner's Best Salsa Meatloaf- A Better Place to Be, 87
Family Taco Night – Common Questions Children Ask About Puberty, 137

German Spaetzle – The Goliath Code, 189
Guinness Chili with Beans – A.K.A., 151
Hint of Summertime Linguini - Smoke in Her Eyes, 175
Honey Rosemary Chicken- The Scribe's Daughter, 33
Hot Dogs – Sofie At Bat, 9
Laughing Cow Peas (pasta) – Trusting the Currents, 95
Lemon Chicken Pita Pockets – Acre's Orphans, 43
Meat Pies – Aerenden: The Child Returns, 21
Medieval Blanc Mange - A King Under Siege, 39
Moroccan Stew – Eva's Secret, 159
Mulligan Stew – Mulligan Stew, 143
Osso Bucco – Vain Pursuits, 133
Panackelty - BLITZ PAM, 47
Apples and Honey Pork Chops – Paradise Girl, 173
Rotisserie Rib Roast on the Grill – To Be a Queen, 69
Spaghetti and Meatballs – Tilly and Torg, 13
Welsh Rarebit – Left Out, 107
Russian Blini with Smoked Salmon- Misha Alexandrov, 111
Trout Almandine – Broken Portal in Rocky Mountain Park, 167
Vegetarian Sushi – The Tempest's Roar, 35

SALAD

Baby Spinach and Chickpea Veggie Salad- In the Hands of Unknown, 75
Kitchari- Mother's Milks, 141
Mandarin Orange Salad with Raspberry Vinaigrette- Curse Breaker, 121
Quinoa, Bean, Corn and Pepper Salad – Betrayal, 119

SOUP

Asparagus Soup – Deadly Affair, 123
Chicken Noodle Soup – In the Comfort of Shadows, 91
Chicken Sausage Gumbo- The Plains of Chalmette, 67
Chilled Cucumber Soup – Veggies Bully, 15
Creamy Mushroom Soup – Mythicals, 171
Lentil and Cabbage Soup - Save Yourself, 145
Tibetan Noodle Soup – The Altitude Journals, 147

VEGETABLES/SIDES

Ants on a Log/ Veggie Dip- Who Knows Jordan?, 17
Cauliflower & Potato Salad – Flux, 161
Chanukah Root Vegetable Latkes – My Magical Kippah, 113
Clapshot – The Covenant Within, 187
Maple Braised Brussels Sprouts with Red Onions- Daisy, Bold & Beautiful, 105
Roasted Potato Lyonnaise – Lady of the Tower, 65
Veggie and Fruit Kabobs – Teddy Tries a Veggie, 11

Expandthetable suggestions for most recipes:

Allium free: Omit onions and garlic

Use ½ fennel bulb, sliced thinly

To make it gluten free, make your own crust with gluten free flour

Egg free: substitute one of the following for the 2 eggs: ½ cup applesauce; ½ cup mashed bananas; ½ cup silken tofu

Vegan –

substitute nondairy substitutes readily available milk – soy, almond

Nondairy cheese

sour cream, butter

Vegetable broth for beef and chicken broth

Sugar Free – Use Stevia or other sugar substitutes

Eat, Read & Dream Cookbook

Geraldine J. Clouston
Susan Weintrob

indieBRAG®

Notes:

- indieBRAG, LLC is a quality standards certification service and all the books in this cookbook have earned the Company's prestigious B.R.A.G. Medallion award. Additional information may be obtained at the Company's website www.bragmedallion.com
- The authors whose books are presented in this cookbook own the copyrights to their respective works.
- Except as noted otherwise, all the recipes provided herein were created by Ms. Susan Weintrob who owns the copyright to these recipes (to the extent such content is copyrightable). Ms. Weintrob has granted indieBRAG a non-exclusive license to include them in this book.
- Except as noted otherwise, Shutterstock holds the copyright on the photographs of food and genre pages contained herein and has granted indieBRAG a non-exclusive right to use them in this book.

Acknowledgments

indieBRAG, LLC wishes to express its sincere gratitude to Ms. Susan Weintrob, a food blogger (expandthetable.net) and culinary expert, who worked tirelessly to develop the recipes contained herein and without whose assistance this book in its current form would not have been possible.

Similarly, indieBRAG, LLC is grateful to all the authors whose B.R.A.G. Medallion honoree books are presented in this cookbook. Through their hard work, persistence and creativity they have written books that are considered worthy of a reader's time and money.

Contents

Welcome to the indieBRAG Eat, Read & Dream Cookbook 1
Children's Genre 2
Fantasy Genre 18
Historical Fiction Genre 36
Horror/Paranormal Genre 70
Literary Fiction Genre 84
Middle Grade Genre 100
Mystery Genre 116
Non-Fiction Genre 134
Romance Genre 148
Science Fiction Genre 164
Thriller Genre 180

Photo courtesy of indieBRAG

Welcome to the indieBRAG Eat, Read & Dream Cookbook

We are excited to bring you this distinctive new cookbook that will appeal to two large and diverse groups of people around the world who like to read books and who like to cook. The common thread that joins them together is the desire to relax, to escape the pressures of everyday life, and to stimulate their imaginations—in other words, to dream.

With that in mind, indieBRAG has brought together an ensemble of award-winning, self-published authors whose books have earned the prestigious B.R.A.G. Medallion and, working with Susan Weintrob, a culinary expert and respected food blogger, we have developed exciting recipes, each of which, springs from the pages of these books and the stories contained therein. Unlike traditional cookbooks, we have grouped these recipes in an unusual and intriguing manner, as each one is presented in concert with the book from which the idea sprung, and all are grouped by each book's literary genre.

In so doing, we have created a cookbook quite different from the thousands of such books that are published each year around the globe. We respectfully submit that our cookbook will take you on a gastronomical and intellectual adventure—one that will entertain you, and teach you, and thereby satisfy both your body and soul. There is truly nothing like it!

So come join us as together we eat, read and dream!

Geraldine J. Clouston
President and C.E.O.
indieBRAG, LLC

Children's Genre

Oh, Susannah: It's in the bag
Banana Bread

Piccadilly and the Jolly Raindrops
Fairy Muffins

Sofie At Bat
Hot Dogs and Toppings

Teddy Tries a Veggie
Veggie and Fruit Kabobs

Tilly and Torg Out to Eat
Spaghetti and Meatballs

Veggie's Bully
Chilled Cucumber Soup

Who Knows Jordan?
Ants on a log